D1133643

# Crochet
## rugs & throws

Hobbs, Janet.
Crochet rugs & throws /

2003.
33305207506837
la          10/18/04

# Crochet
## rugs & throws

### Janet Hobbs

KANGAROO PRESS

SANTA CLARA COUNTY LIBRARY

3 3305 20750 6837

CROCHET RUGS AND THROWS
First published in Australia in 2003 by Kangaroo Press
an imprint of Simon & Schuster (Australia) Pty Ltd,
20 Barcoo Street, East Roseville NSW 2069

A Viacom Company
Sydney  New York  London  Toronto

Visit our website at www.simonsaysaustralia.com

© Copyright Janet Hobbs, 2003

All rights reserved. No part of this publication may be reproduced, sorted in a retrieval system, or transmitted, in any form or by any means, electronic, mechanical, photocopying, recording or otherwise, without the prior permission of the publisher in writing.

The National Library of Australia
Cataloguing-in-Publication data

Hobbs, Janet.
Crochet rugs and throws.

ISBN 0 7318 1150 X.

1. Crocheting — Patterns. 2. Rugs. 3. Afghans (Coverlets).
I. Title.

746.73041

Cover and internal design Anna Warren, Warren Ventures Pty Ltd
Typeset in 10/15 pt Giovanni
Printed in China through Colorcraft Ltd., Hong Kong
10 9 8 7 6 5 4 3 2

# Contents

# Introduction

Crochet is a fine art brought to this country by pioneering women from various parts of the globe. My love of crocheting began when I was 14, growing up in the Australian bush. I started by spending hours unpicking old jumpers and making a rug of a rainbow of colours. I thought it was the most beautiful thing, but my mother obviously didn't think so because the newborn lambs on our farm ended up wearing bits of the rug to keep them warm in winter! My work did develop, though, and six years later I was winning prizes at country shows.

I eventually left home to travel overseas and around Australia, before settling down with my husband, Ralph. With my two kids at school, and the fact that there is no electricity where we live, I thought I'd start my crocheting again, 20 years after winning my first championship. But I couldn't find any books or patterns near my home to help me with new designs, so I thought I would make up my own patterns. Now I am a crochet addict — I just can't stop myself!

One of my favourites is the pale-pink Princess throw featuring white roses, which I made in honour of Diana, Princess of Wales. I'm also a football fan, so I designed a throw using my unique diamond bobble in the colours of my favourite team — of course you can use any colours you like! This will keep the coldest fans warm on a winter night.

My focus with this book is to make the designs attractive, using pure new wool and, above all, easy to follow — I like my work to be very simple. There is certainly something for everyone in this book. I hope you enjoy making the throws and rugs as much as I did designing them.

# Stitches used

I have used the following six crochet stitches in the patterns.

## Chain Stitch

The basic stitch for crocheting.

1   Make a slip knot. Yoh and pull through the slip knot.
2   Yoh and draw yarn through loop.
3   Repeat as many times as required.

## Treble

1  Yoh, then insert hook into 4th chain from hook or where stated in pattern.
2  Draw yarn through making three loops on the hook.
3  Yoh and draw it through the first two loops leaving two loops on hook.
4  Repeat Step 3 leaving one loop on hook.
5  Yoh and insert hook into next chain or where stated in pattern and repeat from Step 2.

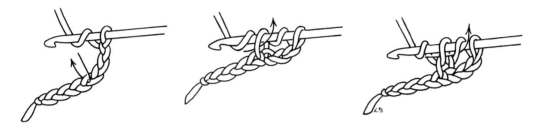

## Half Treble

1  Yoh and inset hook into 3rd chain from hook or where stated in pattern.
2  Yoh and draw through leaving three loops on the hook.
3  Yoh and draw through all three loops leaving one loop.
4  Insert hook into next chain or where stated in pattern and repeat steps 2 and 3.

# Double Treble

1. Yoh twice. Insert the hook in the 5th chain from hook, or where stated in pattern.
2. Yoh once and draw through, leaving four loops on hook.
3. Yoh and draw through two loops leaving three loops on hook.
4. Yoh and draw through two loops leaving two loops on hook.
5. Yoh and draw through two loops leaving one loop on hook.
6. Repeat steps 1 to 5.

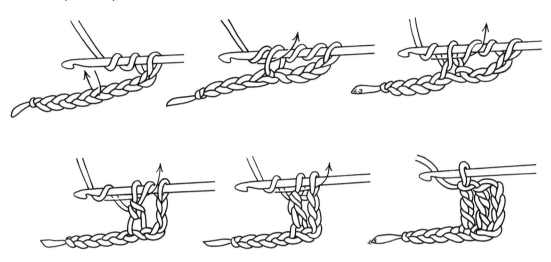

# Double Crochet

1. Insert hook into 2nd chain from hook or where stated in pattern.
2. Yoh and draw loop through leaving 2 loops on hook.
3. Yoh and draw through two loops leaving one loop on hook.
4. Repeat steps 1 to 3.

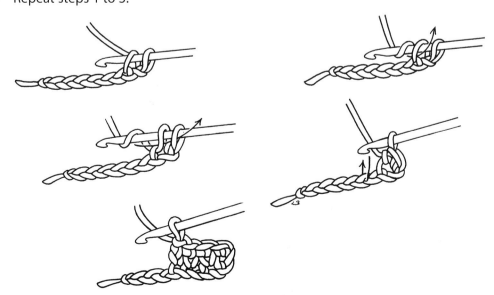

## Slip Stitch

1   Insert hook where stated.
2   Yoh and draw through both loops.

## A note on tension

It is important to follow the gauge given for tension for achieving the right size. Depending on your mood, the tension in your stitching will vary. If you feel tense your crocheting will tend to be tight and then become looser as you relax. To overcome this, some people start with a slightly bigger hook and then when they are relaxed they change to a smaller hook.

## Abbreviations

ch = chain
dc = double crochet
dtr = double treble
htr = half treble
sl st = slip stitch
sp = space
st = stitch
tr = treble
yoh = yarn over hook

| Key | |
|---|---|
| ▲ | bobble |
| \| | treble |
| – – | chain |
| ■ | block |
| O | double crochet |
| Δ | shell |

## A note on graphs

To reduce eyestrain, you may need to enlarge the graphs on a photocopier.

x

# Delicate kisses
## cot cover

*This versatile pure wool cot cover can be used as a baby shawl as well. Delicate and beautiful, it is a delightful mix of pink, lemon, blue and white. Of course, if you have your own favourite colours feel free to substitute them for these colours.*

## Materials

Pure wool 4 ply
Pink 10 × 25g balls
Lemon 6 × 25g balls
Blue 6 × 25g balls
White 15 × 25g balls

*Hook size*: 1.75 mm
*Tension*: 25 trebles to 7.5 cm (3 in) on flat work.

*Note*: You will need to make 10 pink squares, 6 lemon squares, 6 blue squares and 8 white squares (the rest of the white wool is used in the edging).

For the bobble, work 5tr into next st, remove hook from loop, insert hook in first treble of 5tr group then back into loop and draw the loop through the tr, 1ch to fasten off.

Difficulty: *medium*

Ch8, sl st into first ch to form ring.

**Round 1**: 7ch, (1tr 1 bobble 1tr into ring, ch4) 3 times; 1tr 1 bobble into ring, sl st into 3rd ch of 7, sl st across 2ch.

**Round 2**: 7ch, (1tr 1 bobble into corner sp, 1tr into next tr, 2ch, 1tr into next tr, 1tr into each of next 2ch, 4ch) twice; * 1tr 1 bobble into corner sp, 1tr into next tr, 2ch, 1tr into next tr, 2ch, miss 1ch, 1tr into next ch, 4ch; * repeat from * to * once, omitting last tr in ch, sl st into 3rd ch of 7, sl st across 2ch.

**Round 3**: 7ch, (1tr 1 bobble into corner sp 1tr into next tr, 2ch, 1tr in next tr, 1tr into 1ch, miss 1ch, 1tr in each of next 3tr, 1tr in each of next 2ch, 4ch) twice; * 1tr 1 bobble into corner sp, 1tr in next tr, ** 2ch, 1tr into next tr; ** repeat from ** to ** twice, 2ch, miss 1ch, 1tr into next ch, 4ch; * repeat from * to * once, omitting last tr in ch, sl st into 3rd ch of 7, sl st across 2ch.

**Round 4**: 7ch, (1tr 1 bobble into corner sp, 1tr into next tr, 2ch, 1tr in next tr, 1tr into 1ch, miss 1ch, 1tr into each of next 7tr, 1tr into each of next 2ch, 4ch) twice; * 1tr 1 bobble into corner sp, 1tr into next tr, ** 2ch, 1tr into next tr; ** repeat from ** to ** 4 times, 2ch, miss 1ch, 1tr into next ch, 4ch; * repeat from * to * once, omitting last tr in ch, sl st into 3rd ch of 7, sl st across 2ch.

**Round 5**: 7ch, (1tr 1 bobble into corner sp, 1tr into next tr, 2ch, 1tr into next tr, 1tr into ch, miss 1ch, 1tr into each of next 11tr, 1tr into each of next 2ch, 4ch) twice; * 1tr 1 bobble into corner sp, 1tr into next tr, ** 2ch, 1tr into next tr; ** repeat from ** to ** 6 times, 2ch, miss 1ch, 1tr into next ch, 4ch; * repeat from * to * once, omitting last tr in ch, sl st into 3rd ch of 7, sl st across 2ch.

**Round 6**: 7ch, (1tr 1 bobble into corner sp, 1tr into next tr, 2ch, 1tr in next tr, 1tr in ch, miss 1ch, 1tr into each of next 15tr, 1tr into each of next 2ch, 4ch) twice; * 1tr 1 bobble into corner sp, 1tr into next tr, ** 2ch, 1tr into next tr; ** repeat from ** to ** 8 times, 2ch, miss 1ch, 1tr into next ch, 4ch; * repeat from * to * once, omitting last tr in ch, sl st into 3rd ch of 7, sl st across 2ch.

**Round 7**: 7ch, (1tr 1 bobble into corner sp 1tr into next tr, 2ch, 1tr into next tr, 1tr in ch, miss 1ch, 1tr into each of next 19tr, 1tr into each of next 2ch, 4ch) twice; * 1tr 1 bobble into corner sp, 1tr into next tr, ** 2ch, 1tr into next tr; ** repeat from ** to ** 10 times, 2ch, miss 1ch, 1tr into next ch, 4ch; * repeat from * to * once, omitting last tr in ch, sl st into 3rd ch of 7, sl st across 2ch.

**Round 8**: 7ch, (1tr 1 bobble into corner sp, 1tr into next tr, 2ch, 1tr into next tr, 1tr into ch, miss 1ch, 1tr into each of next 23tr, 1tr into each of next 2ch, 4ch) twice; * 1tr 1 bobble into corner sp, 1tr into next tr, ** 2ch, 1tr into next tr; ** repeat from ** to ** 12 times, 2ch, miss 1ch, 1tr into next ch, 4ch; * repeat from * to * once, omitting last tr in ch, sl st into 3rd ch of 7, sl st across 2ch.

**Round 9**: 7ch, (1tr 1 bobble into corner sp, 1tr into next tr, 2ch, 1tr into next tr, 1tr into 1ch, miss 1ch, 1tr into each of next 27tr, 1tr into each of next 2ch, 4ch) twice; * 1tr 1 bobble into corner sp, 1tr into next tr, ** 2ch, 1tr into next tr; ** repeat from ** to ** 14 times, 2ch, miss 1ch, 1tr in next ch, 4ch; * repeat from * to * once, omitting last tr in ch, sl st into 3rd ch of 7, sl st across 2ch.

**Round 10**: 7ch, (1tr 1 bobble into corner sp, 1tr into next tr, 2ch, 1tr into next tr, 1tr into 1ch, miss 1ch, 1tr into each of next 31tr, 1tr into each of next 2ch, 4ch) twice; * 1tr 1 bobble into corner sp, 1tr into next tr, ** 2ch, 1tr into next tr; ** repeat from ** to ** 16 times, 2ch, miss 1ch, 1tr into next ch, 4ch; * repeat from * to * once, omitting last tr in ch, sl st into 3rd ch of 7, sl st across 2ch.

| WHITE | BLUE | PINK | LEMON | WHITE |
|---|---|---|---|---|
| PINK | WHITE | BLUE | PINK | LEMON |
| LEMON | PINK | WHITE | BLUE | PINK |
| PINK | BLUE | WHITE | PINK | LEMON |
| LEMON | PINK | BLUE | WHITE | PINK |
| WHITE | LEMON | PINK | BLUE | WHITE |

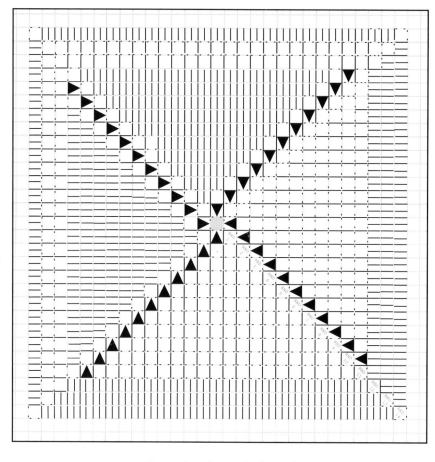

**Round 11**: 7ch, (1tr 1 bobble into corner sp, 1tr into next tr, 2ch, 1tr into next tr, 1tr into 1ch, miss 1ch, 1tr into each of next 35tr, 1tr into each of next 2ch, 4ch) twice; * 1tr 1 bobble into corner sp, 1tr into next tr, ** 2ch, 1tr into next tr; ** repeat from ** to ** 18 times, 2ch, miss 1ch, 1tr into next ch, 4ch; * repeat from * to * once, omitting last tr in ch, sl st into 3rd ch of 7, sl st across 2ch.

**Round 12**: 7ch, (1tr into next ch, 2ch, miss 1ch, 1tr into next tr, 2ch, 1tr into next tr, 2ch, miss 2ch, 1tr into next tr, ** 2ch, miss 1tr, 1tr into next tr; ** repeat from ** to ** 18 times, 2ch, miss 1ch, 1tr into next ch, 4ch) twice; * 1tr into each of next 2ch, 1tr in next tr, 1tr in next tr, ** 1tr in 1ch, miss 1ch, 1tr in next tr; ** repeat from ** to ** 19 times, 1tr in each of next 2ch, 4ch; * repeat from * to * once, omitting last tr in ch, sl st into 3rd ch of 7, sl st across 2ch.

**Round 13**: 7ch, (1tr into next ch, 2ch, miss 1ch, 1tr into next tr, ** 2ch, 1tr into next tr; ** repeat from ** to ** 22 times, 2ch, miss 1ch, 1tr into next ch, 4ch) twice; * 1tr in each of next 2ch, 1tr into each of next 46tr, 1tr into each of next 2ch, 4ch; * repeat from * to * once, omitting last tr in ch, sl st into 3rd ch of 7. Fasten off.

**Round 14** is worked in white, join in wool at the second ch of the corner, 7ch, (1tr into each of next 2ch, 1tr into next tr, ** 1tr into next ch, miss 1ch, 1tr into next tr; ** repeat from ** to ** 24 times, 1tr into each of next 2ch, 4ch) twice; * 1tr into each of next 2ch, 1tr into each tr to corner, 1tr into each of next 2ch, 4ch; * repeat from * to * once, omitting last tr in ch, sl st into 3rd ch of 7. Fasten off.

With right sides together, sew squares together, referring to the graph above. Edging is worked in white.

Join in wool in a corner sp, 1ch, 3dc, 5ch, sl st into the first ch of 5 to form picot, work 5dc, 5ch, sl st into first ch of 5, work 5dc and 5ch picot all the way around cot cover to beginning of round, sl st into 1ch at beginning of round.

# Princess white roses knee rug

White roses were Princess Diana's favourite flowers and she was also known as England's rose. So it became a quest of mine to design a rug to reflect both her femininity and her beauty. Using pure wool to make both the white roses and the pale pink of the surrounds, I hope this rug will ensure that her memory lives on for those who make it.

## Materials

Pure wool 5 ply
Pink 30 × 50g balls
Maroon 1 × 50g ball
White 6 × 50g balls

*Hook sizes*: 3.00 mm; 1.75 mm
*Tension*: 21 trebles to 7.5 cm (3 in) over flat work.

*Note*: For the bobble, work 5tr into next st, remove hook from loop, insert hook in first tr of 5tr group then back into loop and draw the loop through the tr, 1ch to fasten off.

Difficulty: *medium*

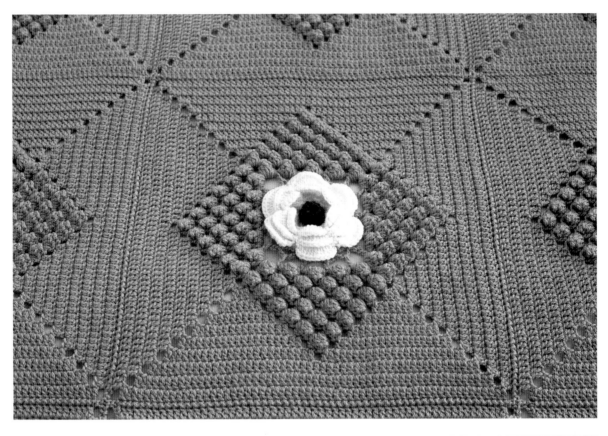

## *White roses*

Work the white roses with the 1.75 mm hook. Ch6, sl st into first ch to form ring.

**Round 1**: 8ch, (1tr into ring, 5ch) 5 times; sl st into the 3rd ch of 8.

**Round 2**: 1ch, (work 1dc 1htr 3tr 1htr 1dc into 5ch loop, work a sl st into next tr) 6 times; omitting sl st into next tr, sl st into 1ch at beginning of round.

**Round 3**: 7ch, (work a sl st into the sl st of last round, 6ch) 5 times; sl st into the first ch of 7.

**Round 4**: 1ch, (work 1dc 1htr 5tr 1htr 1dc into 6ch loop, sl st into sl st of previous round) 6 times; remember to work a sl st into the 1ch at beginning of round.

**Round 5**: 8ch, (sl st into sl st of previous round, 7ch) 5 times; sl st into into first ch of 8.

**Round 6**: 1ch, (work 1dc 1htr 7tr 1htr 1dc into 7ch loop, sl st into sl st of previous round) 6 times; remember to sl st into 1ch at beginning of round.

**Round 7**: ch9, (sl st into sl st of previous round, 8ch) 5 times; sl st into the first ch of 9.

**Round 8**: 1ch, (work 1dc 1htr 9tr 1htr 1dc into 8ch loop, sl st into sl st of previous round) 6 times; sl st into 1ch at beginning of round. Fasten off.

## *To make the rug*

Change to 3.00 mm hook. (3ch counts as 1tr.)

Join pink wool into a sl st of the last round of the rose, and work as follows.

**Round 1**: ch9, (sl st into the next sl st of previous round of the rose, ch9) 5 times; sl st into the first ch of 9.

**Round 2**: sl st into 9ch loop, into the same loop work (1dc, 5ch, 1dc, 5ch, 1dc, 5ch), into each of next 3 loops work (1dc, 5ch, 1dc, 5ch, 1dc, 5ch), into the 5th loop work (1dc, 5ch, 1dc, 5ch), into the last loop work (1dc, 5ch, 1dc, 5ch), sl st into the dc at the beginning of the round, you should have 16 spaces.

**Round 3**: sl st into middle of first 5ch loop, 7ch, (1tr into next sp, 4ch); repeat to end, sl st into 3rd ch of 7, you should still have 16 spaces.

**Round 4**: sl st across 2ch, 7ch, 1tr 1 bobble 1tr into same sp (2ch 1tr 1 bobble 1tr into next sp) 4 times; 4ch, 1tr 1 bobble 1tr into the same sp as last bobble, this is the first corner, 4 times; 4ch, 1tr 1 bobble 1tr into same sp as last bobble, this is the 2nd corner, 4 times; 4ch, 1tr 1 bobble 1tr into the same sp as the last bobble, this is the 3rd corner; 4 times; sl st into the 3rd ch of 7, this is the 4th corner, sl st across 2ch.

**Round 5**: 7ch, (1tr 1 bobble into corner sp, 1tr in next tr, * 2ch, 1tr in next tr, 1 bobble into 2ch sp, 1tr in next tr; * repeat from * to * 3 times, 2ch, 1tr in next tr, 1 bobble 1 tr into 4 ch sp, 4ch); repeat to end, omitting the last tr, sl st into the 3rd ch of 7, sl st across 2ch.

**Round 6**: 7ch, (1tr in each of next 2ch, 1tr in next tr, 2ch, * 1tr in next tr, 1 bobble in 2ch sp, 1tr in next tr, 2ch; * repeat from * to * 4 times, 1tr in next tr, 1tr in each of next 2ch, 4ch); repeat to end, omitting last tr in ch, sl st into 3rd ch of 7, sl st across 2ch.

**Round 7**: 7ch, (1tr in each of next 2ch, 1tr in each of next 3tr, 1tr in 1ch, miss 1ch, 1tr in next tr, 2ch, * 1tr in next tr, 1 bobble in 2ch sp, 1tr in next tr, 2ch; * repeat from * to * 3 times, 1tr in next tr, 1tr in 1ch, miss 1ch, 1tr in each of next 3tr, 1tr in each of next 2ch, 4ch); repeat to end, omitting last tr in ch, sl st into 3rd ch of 7, sl st across 2ch.

**Round 8**: 7ch, (1tr in each of next 2ch, 1tr in each of next 7tr, 1tr in 1ch, miss 1ch, 1tr in next tr, 2ch, * 1tr in next tr, 1 bobble in 2ch sp, 1tr in next tr, 2ch; * repeat from * to * twice, 1tr in next tr, 1tr in 1ch, miss 1ch, 1tr in each of next 7tr, 1tr in each of next 2ch, 4ch); repeat to end, sl st into 3rd ch of 7, sl st across 2ch.

**Round 9**: 7ch, (1tr in each of next 2ch, 1tr in each of next 11tr, 1tr in 1ch, miss 1ch, 1tr in next tr, 2ch, * 1tr in next tr, 1 bobble in 2ch sp, 1tr in next tr, 2ch; * repeat from * to * once, 1tr in next tr, 1tr in 1ch, miss 1ch, 1tr in each of next 11tr, 1tr in each of next 2ch, 4ch); repeat to end, sl st into 3rd ch of 7, sl st across 2ch.

**Round 10**: 7ch, (1tr in each of next 2ch, 1tr in each of next 15tr, 1tr in 1ch, miss 1ch, 1tr in next tr 2ch, 1tr in next tr, 1 bobble in 2ch sp, 1tr in next tr, 2ch, 1tr in next tr, 1tr in 1ch, miss 1ch, 1tr in each of next 15tr, 1tr in each of next 2ch, 4ch); repeat to end, sl st into 3rd ch of 7, sl st across 2ch.

**Round 11**: 7ch, (1tr in each of next 2ch, 1tr in each of next 19tr, 1tr in 1ch, miss 1ch, 1tr in next tr, 2ch, 1tr in next tr, 1tr in 1ch, miss 1ch, 1tr in each of next 19tr, 1tr in each of next 2ch, 4ch); repeat to end, sl st into 3rd ch of 7, sl st across 2ch.

**Round 12**: 7ch, (1tr in each of next 2ch, 1tr in each of next 23tr, miss 1ch, 1tr in next ch, 1tr in each of next 23tr, 1tr in each of next 2ch, 4ch); repeat to end, sl st into 3rd ch of 7, sl st across 2ch.

**Round 13**: 7ch, (1tr in each of next 2ch, 1tr in each of next 51tr, 1tr in each of next 2ch, 4ch); repeat to end, sl st into 3rd ch of 7, sl st across 2ch.

**Round 14**: 7ch, (1tr in each of next 2ch, 1tr in each of next 55tr, 1tr in each of next 2ch, 4ch); repeat to end, sl st into 3rd ch of 7. Fasten off.

Use maroon wool for the centre of the rose. Ch6, sl st into first ch to form loop, 2ch, work 10htr into loop, sl st into second ch at the beginning of round. Fasten off.

## Backing

For white backing on white roses, use white wool, 6ch, sl st into first ch to form loop.

**Round 1**: 7ch, (3tr into loop, 4ch) 3 times; 2tr into loop, sl st into 3rd ch of 7, sl st across 2ch.

**Round 2**: 7ch, (1tr into each of next 2ch, 1tr into each of next 3tr, 1tr into each of next 2ch, 4ch); repeat to end, sl st into 3rd ch of 7, sl st across 2ch.

**Round 3**: 7ch, (1tr into each of next 2ch, 1tr into each of next 7tr, 1tr into each of next 2ch, [11 trebles] 4ch); repeat to end, sl st into 3rd ch of 7. Fasten off.

To make up, join the squares by sewing tr to tr; there are 5 squares to a row with 25 squares in all. Using maroon wool sew maroon centre into the centre of the white roses, sew the backs on the white roses last, making sure they are square and even.

Bobble edging is worked in white. For bobble edging join in wool at a corner sp, work 1dc into same sp, 4ch, work a bobble into 1dc, 1dc into first tr from hook, 4ch, work a bobble into 1dc, 1dc into 3rd tr from hook, 4ch, 1 bobble into 1dc, 1dc into 3rd tr from hook, 4ch, 1 bobble into 1dc; repeat all the way around rug, working 2 bobbles into corner spaces, work 1dc 4ch 1 bobble into corner where you started, then sl st into dc at start of round. Fasten off.

# Federation
## throw rug

*This rug is an easy design for the less experienced. It is made of pure wool and can also be used as a cot cover or a floor rug. You can make this rug as small or as big as you wish.*

## Materials

Pure wool 8 ply
Green 40 × 50g balls
Gold 30 × 50g balls

*Hook size*: 3.00 mm
*Tension*: 24 trebles to 10 cm (4 in) over flat work.

*Note*: You will need to make 36 green squares and 25 gold squares.

For the bobble, work 5tr in next st, remove hook from loop, insert hook in first tr of 5tr group then back into loop and draw the loop through the tr, 1ch to fasten off.

Difficulty: *easy*

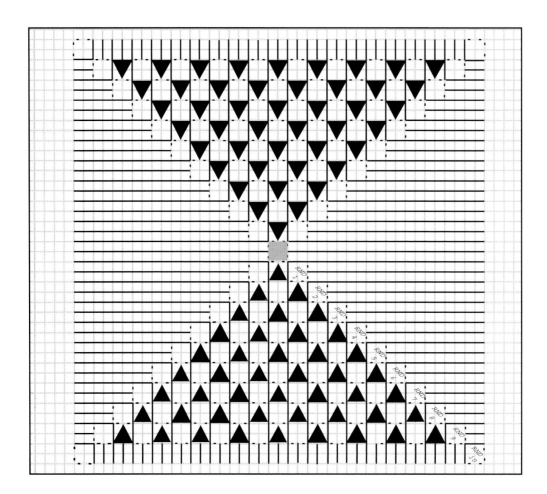

Make 8ch, sl st into first ch to form ring.

**Round 1**: 7ch, (1tr 1 bobble 1tr into ring, 4ch, 3tr into ring, 4ch) twice; working only 2tr in ring instead of 3; sl st into 3rd ch of 7, that makes the 3rd tr, then sl st across 2ch.

**Round 2**: 7ch, (1tr 1 bobble in corner sp, 1tr in next tr, 2ch, 1tr in next tr, 1 bobble 1tr in corner sp, 4ch, 2tr in corner sp, 1tr in each of next 3tr, 2tr in corner sp, 4ch) twice; working only 6tr instead of 7, sl st into 3rd ch of 7, that makes the 7th tr, sl st across 2ch.

**Round 3**: 7ch, (1tr 1 bobble in corner sp, 1tr in next tr, 2ch, 1tr in next tr, 1 bobble in 2ch sp, 1tr in next tr, 2ch, 1tr in next tr 1 bobble 1tr in corner sp, 4ch, 2tr in corner sp, 1tr in each of next 7tr, 2tr in corner sp, [11 trebles worked] 4ch) twice; working 10tr, sl st into 3rd ch of 7, sl st across 2ch.

**Round 4**: 7ch, (1tr 1 bobble in corner sp, 1tr in next tr, 2ch, * 1tr in next tr, 1 bobble in 2ch sp, 1tr in next tr, 2ch; * repeat from * to * once, 1tr in next tr, 1 bobble 1tr in corner, 4ch, 2tr in corner sp, 1tr in each of next 11tr, 2tr in corner sp, [15 trebles worked] 4ch) twice, omitting last tr in corner sp; 14tr worked, last tr is worked, sl st into 3rd ch of 7, sl st across 2ch.

**Round 5**: 7ch, (1tr 1 bobble in corner sp, 1tr in next tr, 2ch, * 1tr in next tr, 1 bobble in 2ch sp, 1tr in next tr, 2ch; * repeat from * to * twice, 1tr in next tr, 1 bobble 1tr in corner sp, 4ch, 2tr in corner sp, 1tr in each of next 15tr, 2tr in corner, [19 trebles] 4ch) twice; working 18tr, sl st into 3rd ch of 7 makes last tr, sl st across 2ch.

**Round 6**: 7ch, (1tr 1 bobble in corner, 1tr in next tr, 2ch, * 1tr in next tr, 1 bobble in 2ch sp, 1tr in next tr, 2ch; * repeat from * to * 3 times, 1tr in next tr, 1 bobble, 1tr in corner, 4ch, 2tr in corner sp, 1tr in each 19tr, 2tr in corner sp, [23 trebles] 4ch) twice; omitting last tr, sl st into 3rd ch of 7, sl st across 2ch.

**Round 7**: 7ch, (1tr 1 bobble in corner sp, 1tr in next tr, 2ch, * 1tr in next tr, 1 bobble in 2ch sp, 1tr in next tr, 2ch; * repeat from * to * 4 times, 1tr in next tr, 1 bobble 1tr in corner, 4ch, 2tr in corner, 1tr in each of next 23tr, 2tr in corner sp, [27 trebles] 4ch) twice; omitting last tr; sl st into 3rd ch of 7, sl st across 2ch.

**Round 8**: 7ch, (1tr 1 bobble in corner, 1tr in next tr, 2ch, * 1tr in next tr, 1 bobble in 2ch sp, 1tr in next tr, 2ch; * repeat from * to * 5 times, 1tr in next tr, 1 bobble 1tr in corner sp, 4ch, 2tr in corner, 1tr in each of next 27tr, 2tr in corner sp, [31 trebles] 4ch) twice; omitting last tr; sl st into 3rd ch of 7, sl st across 2ch.

**Round 9**: 7ch, (1tr 1 bobble in corner sp, 1tr in next tr, 2ch, * 1tr, in next tr, 1 bobble in 2ch sp, 1tr in next tr, 2ch; * repeat from * to * 6 times, 1tr in next

tr, 1 bobble 1tr in corner sp, 4ch, 2tr in corner sp, 1tr in each of next 31tr, 2tr in corner sp, [35 trebles] 4ch) twice; omitting last tr; sl st into 3rd ch of 7, sl st across 2ch.

**Round 10**: 7ch, 1tr in each of next 2ch, (1tr in next tr, 1tr in 1ch of bobble 1tr in next tr, 1tr in ch, miss 1ch); repeat to corner, work 1tr in each of next 2ch, [39 trebles worked along one side] 4ch); repeat to end making sure that there are 39 trebles on all sides, sl st into 3rd ch of 7, fasten off.

To join squares together, with right sides together use green or gold wool and flat sew st for st to give a neat finish.

For bobble edging join gold wool in a corner sp, work a dc into same sp, 4ch, 1 bobble in dc, in third tr from hook work 1dc, 4ch, 1 bobble in dc, in third tr from hook work 1dc, 4ch, 1 bobble in dc; repeat all the way around rug, sl st into dc at beginning of round, remembering to work 2 bobbles in corner spaces.

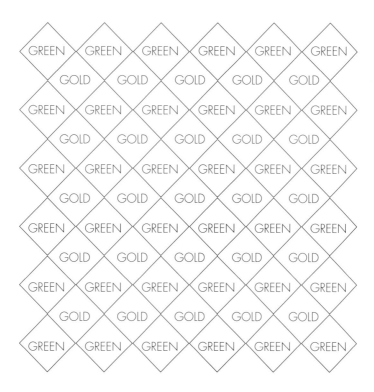

# Coloured bobble
## knee rug

*When I started designing my own patterns I often didn't have a clear idea of what I was going to do. The pattern would unfold as I worked. This knee rug was the very first pattern I designed. When I started I knew I wanted something different and colourful and this is the result. Made from pure wool, use any colours you like and make it as big or small as you like. By adding more squares turn it into a bed spread or reduce the number of squares and produce a cushion cover.*

## Materials

Pure wool 8 ply
White 20 × 50g balls
Cream 20 × 50g balls
Blue 5 × 50g balls
Red 3 × 50g balls
Light green 4 × 50g balls
Burgundy 3 × 50g balls
Dark green 5 × 50g balls

*Hook size*: 3.00 mm
*Tension*: 24 trebles over 10 cm (4 in) of flat work.

Difficulty: *easy*

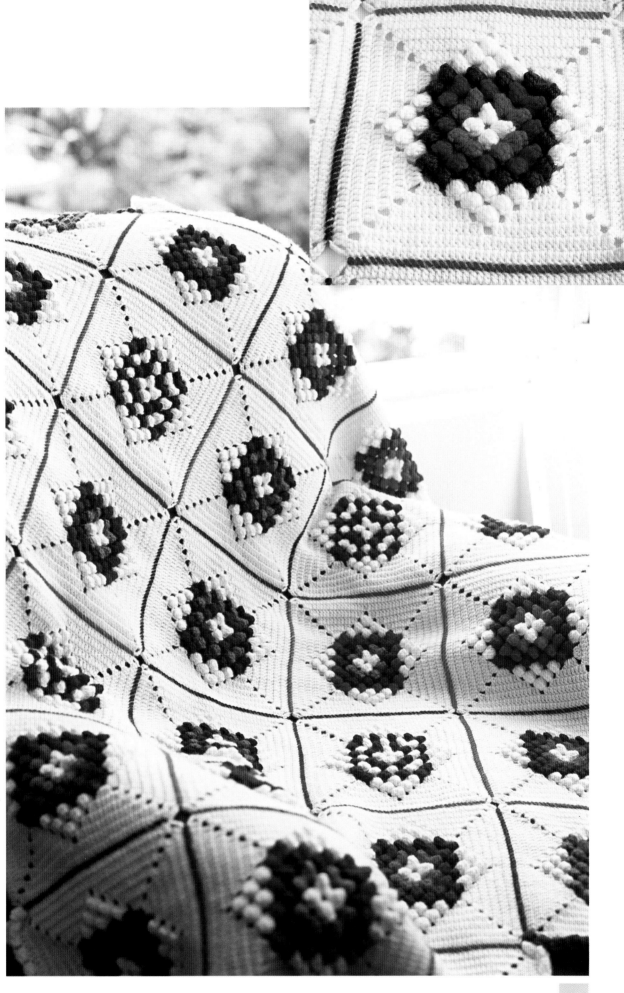

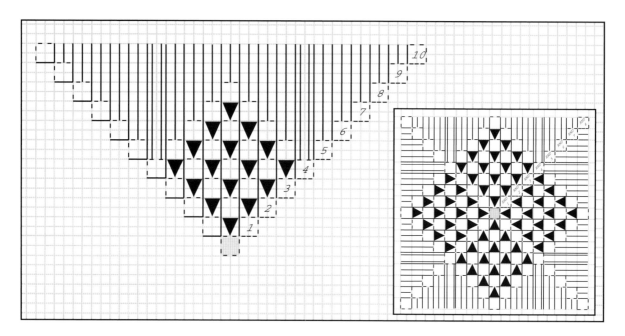

Notes: Squares are as follows.

A: white centre, round dark green, round blue, round light green, rest white. Make 4.

B: white centre, round dark green, round light green, round burgundy, rest white. Make 9.

C: cream centre, round dark green, round blue, round light green, rest cream. Make 4.

D: cream centre, round light green, round burgundy, round red, rest cream. Make 6.

E: cream centre, round blue, round red, round dark green, rest cream. Make 8.

F: white centre, round blue, round red, round dark green, rest white. Make 4.

G: white centre, round dark green, round white, round dark green, rest white. Make 4.

H: cream centre, round dark green, round light green, round burgundy, rest cream. Make 2.

For the bobble, work 5tr in next st, remove hook from loop, insert hook in first of 5tr group then back into loop and draw the loop through the tr, 1ch to fasten off.

Make 8ch, sl st into first ch to form ring.

**Round 1**: 7ch, (1tr 1 bobble 1tr into ring, 4ch) 3 times; 1tr 1 bobble into ring, omitting last tr, this is worked by, sl st into 3rd ch of 7, sl st across 2ch.

**Round 2**: 7ch, (1tr 1 bobble into corner sp, 1tr in next tr, 2ch, 1tr in next tr, 1 bobble 1tr in corner sp, 4ch); repeat to end, omitting last tr in corner sp, sl st into 3rd ch of 7, sl st across 2ch.

**Round 3**: 7ch, (1tr 1 bobble into corner sp, 1tr in next tr, 2ch, 1tr in next tr, 1 bobble in 2ch sp, 1tr in next tr, 2ch, 1tr in next tr 1 bobble 1tr in corner sp, 4ch); repeat to end, omitting last tr in corner sp, sl st into 3rd ch of 7, sl st across 2ch.

**Round 4**: 7ch, (1tr 1 bobble in corner sp, 1tr in next tr, 2ch, * 1tr in next tr, 1 bobble in 2ch sp, ltr in next tr, 2ch; * repeat from * to * once, 1tr in next tr, 1 bobble 1tr in corner sp, 4ch); repeat to end, omitting last tr in corner sp, sl st into 3rd ch of 7, sl st across 2ch.

**Round 5**: 7ch, (3tr into corner sp, 1tr in next tr, [4 trebles worked] 2ch, * 1tr in next tr, 1 bobble in 2ch sp, 1tr in next tr, 2ch; * repeat from * to *

twice, 1tr in next tr, 3tr in corner sp [4 trebles] 4ch); repeat to end, omitting last tr in corner sp, sl st into 3rd ch of 7, sl st across 2ch.

**Round 6**: 7ch, (2tr in corner, 1tr in each of next 4tr, 1tr in 1ch, miss 1ch, 1tr in next tr, [8 treble worked] 2ch, 1tr in next tr, 1 bobble in 2ch sp, 1tr in next tr, 2ch, 1tr in next tr, 1 bobble in 2ch sp, 1tr in next tr, 2ch, 1tr in next tr, 1tr in 1ch, miss 1ch, 1tr in each of next 4tr, 2tr in corner sp, 4ch); repeat to end, omitting last tr in corner sp, sl st into 3rd ch of 7, sl st across 2ch.

**Round 7**: 7ch, (2tr in corner sp, 1tr in each of next 8tr, 1tr in 1ch, miss 1ch, 1tr in next tr, 2ch, 1tr in next tr, 1 bobble in 2ch sp, 1tr in next tr, 2ch, 1tr in next tr, 1tr in 1ch, miss 1ch, 1tr in each of next 8tr, 2tr in corner sp, [12 trebles worked] 4ch); repeat to end, omitting last tr, sl st into 3rd ch of 7, sl st across 2ch.

**Round 8**: 7ch, (2tr in corner sp, 1tr in each of next 12tr, 1tr in 1ch, miss 1ch, 1tr in next tr [16 trebles worked], 2ch, 1tr in next tr, 1tr in 1ch, miss 1ch, 1tr in each of next 12 tr, 2tr in corner sp [16 treble], 4ch); repeat to end, omitting last tr in corner sp, sl st across 2ch.

**Round 9**: 7ch, (2tr in corner sp, 1tr in each of next 16tr, 1tr in 1ch, miss 1ch, 1tr in each of next 16tr, 2tr in corner sp [37 trebles worked] 4ch); repeat to end, omitting last tr in corner sp, sl st into 3rd ch of 7, sl st across 2ch.

**Round 10**: 7ch, (2tr in corner sp, 1tr in each of next 37tr, 2tr in corner sp [41 treble], 4ch); repeat to end, sl st into 3rd ch of 7. Fasten off.

To join the squares use different colours and with right sides together sew tr to tr; repeat on reverse side to give a Royal Show finish. Refer to graph insert on page 16.

For the bobble edging use any colour you like. Join wool in a corner sp, work a dc into same sp, 4ch, 1 bobble into dc, dc into first tr at corner sp, 4ch, 1 bobble into dc, dc into 3rd tr from hook, 4ch, 1 bobble into dc (dc into 3rd tr from hook, 4ch, 1 bobble into dc); repeat all the way around rug working 2 bobbles in corner spaces, work 1 bobble into corner sp at beginning of round sl st into first dc. Fasten off.

# Royal thistle
## cot cover

*I was inspired to design this cot cover when I saw the Duchess of York wearing her beautiful wedding gown featuring Prince Andrew's royal emblem, the thistle. This beautiful cot cover made from pure wool is indeed fit for a baby prince or princess!*

## Materials

Pure wool 4 ply
Cream 60 × 25g balls

*Hook size*: 1.75 mm
*Tension*: 23 treble to 10 cm (4 in) over flat work.

*Note*: For the bobble, work 5tr into next st, remove hook from loop, insert hook in first tr of 5tr group then back into loop and draw the loop through the tr, 1ch to fasten off.

Block is worked (3tr), plus 2tr for each additional block in group.

Picot: 5ch, sl st into first ch.

Difficulty: *hard*

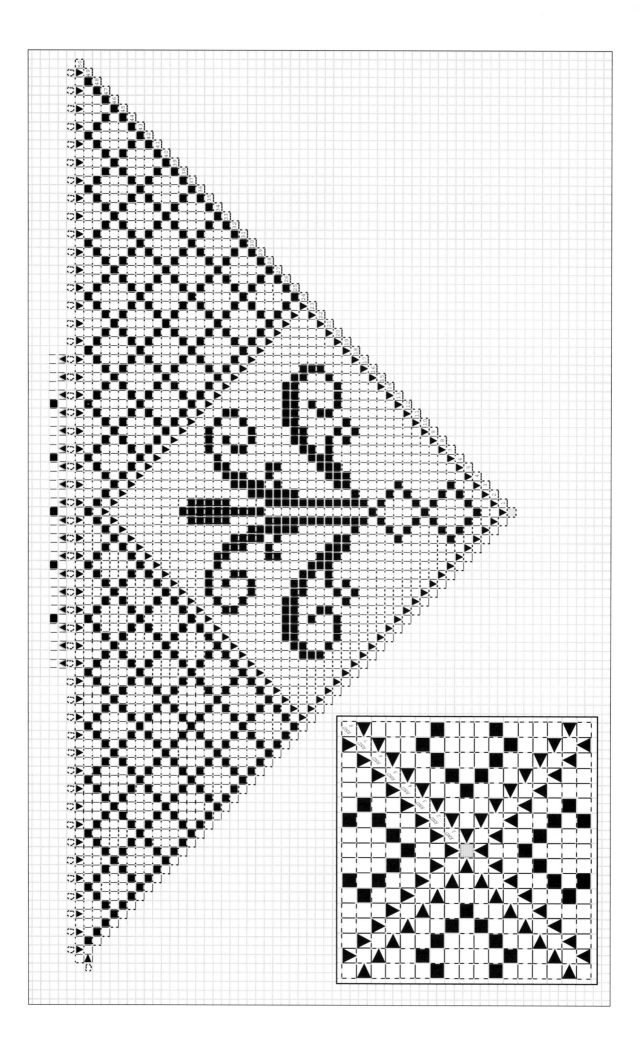

Make 8ch, sl st into first ch to form ring.

**Round 1**: 7ch, (1tr 1 bobble 1tr into ring, 4ch); 3 times; 1tr 1 bobble into ring, sl st into 3rd ch of 7, this makes the last tr, sl st across 2ch.

**Round 2**: 7ch, (1tr 1 bobble into corner sp 1tr in next tr, 2ch, 1tr in next tr, 1 bobble 1tr into corner sp, 4ch); repeat to end, omitting last tr and 4ch, sl st into 3rd ch of 7, sl st across 2ch.

**Round 3**: 7ch, (1tr 1 bobble into corner sp, * 1tr in next tr, 2ch; * repeat from * to * twice, 1tr in next tr, 1 bobble 1tr into corner sp, 4ch); repeat to end, omitting last tr and 4ch, sl st into 3rd ch of 7, sl st across 2ch.

**Round 4**: 7ch, (1tr 1 bobble into corner sp, 1tr in next tr, 2ch, 1tr in next tr, 2ch, 1 block, 2ch, 1tr in next tr, 2ch, 1tr in next tr, 1 bobble 1tr into corner sp, 4ch); repeat to end, omitting last tr and 4ch, sl st into 3rd ch of 7, sl st across 2ch.

**Round 5**: 7ch, (1tr 1 bobble into corner sp, * 1tr into next tr 2ch; * repeat from * to * once, 1 block, 2ch 1 block, ** 2ch, 1tr in next tr; ** repeat from ** to ** once, 1 bobble 1tr into corner sp, 4ch); repeat to end, omitting last tr and 4ch, sl st into 3rd ch of 7, sl st across 2ch.

**Round 6**: 7ch, (1tr 1 bobble into corner sp, ** 1tr in next tr, 2ch; ** repeat from ** to ** once, 1 block, * 2ch, 1tr in next tr; * repeat from * to * once, 2ch, 1 block; repeat from * to * twice, 1 bobble 1tr into corner sp, 4ch); repeat to end, omitting last tr and 4ch, sl st into 3rd ch of 7, sl st across 2ch.

**Round 7**: 7ch, (1tr 1 bobble into corner sp, ** 1tr in next tr, 2ch; ** repeat from ** to ** once, 1 block, * 2ch, 1tr in next tr; * repeat from * to * 3 times, 2ch, 1 block; repeat from * to * twice, 1 bobble 1tr into corner sp, 4ch); repeat to end, omitting last tr and 4ch, sl st into 3rd ch of 7, sl st across 2ch.

**Round 8**: 7ch, (1tr 1 bobble into corner sp, ** 1tr in next tr, 2ch; ** repeat from ** to ** 3 times, 1 block, * 2ch, 1tr in next tr; * repeat from * to * once, 2ch, 1 block; repeat from * to * 4 times, 1 bobble 1tr into corner sp, 4ch); repeat to end, omitting last tr and 4ch, sl st into 3rd ch of 7, sl st across 2ch.

**Round 9**: 7ch, (1tr 1 bobble into corner sp, ** 1tr in next tr, 2ch; ** repeat from ** to ** 5 times, 1 block, 2ch, 1 block, * 2ch, 1tr in next tr; * repeat from * to * 5 times, 1 bobble 1tr into corner sp, 4ch); repeat to end, omitting last tr and 4ch, sl st into 3rd ch of 7, sl st across 2ch.

**Round 10**: 7ch, (1tr 1 bobble into corner sp, ** 1tr in next tr, 2ch; ** repeat from ** to ** 6 times, 1tr in next tr, 2ch, 1 block, * 2ch, 1tr in next tr; * repeat from * to * 7 times, 1 bobble 1tr into corner sp, 4ch); repeat to end, omitting last tr and 4ch, sl st into 3rd ch of 7, sl st across 2ch.

**Round 11**: 7ch, (1tr 1 bobble into corner sp, ** 1tr in next tr, 2ch; ** repeat from ** to ** 7 times, 1 block, 2ch, 1 block, * 2ch, 1tr in next tr; * repeat from * to * 7 times, 1 bobble 1tr into corner sp, 4ch); repeat to end, omitting last tr and 4ch, sl st into 3rd ch of 7, sl st across 2ch.

**Round 12**: 7ch, (1tr 1 bobble into corner sp, ** 1tr in next tr, 2ch; ** repeat from ** to ** 7 times, 1 block, * 2ch, 1tr in next tr; * repeat from * to * once, 2ch, 1 block; repeat from * to * 8 times, 1 bobble 1tr into corner sp, 4ch); repeat to end, omitting last tr and 4ch, sl st into 3rd ch of 7, sl st across 2ch.

**Round 13**: 7ch, (1tr 1 bobble into corner sp, ** 1tr in next tr, 2ch; ** repeat from ** to ** 7 times, 1 block, * 2ch, 1tr in next tr; * repeat from * to *

3 times, 2ch, 1 block; repeat from * to * 8 times, 1 bobble 1tr into corner sp, 4ch); repeat to end, omitting last tr and 4ch, sl st into 3rd ch of 7, sl st across 2ch.

**Round 14**: 7ch, (1tr 1 bobble into corner sp, ** 1tr in next tr, 2ch; ** repeat from ** to ** 9 times, 1 block, * 2ch, 1tr in next tr; * repeat from * to * once, 2ch, 1 block; repeat from * to * 10 times, 1 bobble 1tr in corner sp, 4ch); repeat to end, omitting last tr and 4ch, sl st into 3rd ch of 7, sl st across 2ch.

**Round 15**: 7ch, (1tr 1 bobble into corner sp, ** 1tr in next tr, 2ch; ** repeat from ** to ** 11 times, 1 block, 2ch, 1 block, * 2ch, 1tr in next tr; * repeat from * to * 11 times, 1 bobble 1tr into corner sp, 4ch); repeat to end, omitting last tr and 4ch, sl st into 3rd ch of 7, sl st across 2ch.

**Round 16**: 7ch, (1tr 1 bobble into corner sp, ** 1tr in next tr, 2ch; ** repeat from ** to ** 13 times, 1 block, * 2ch, 1tr in next tr; * repeat from * to * 13 times, 1 bobble 1tr into corner sp, 4ch); repeat to end, omitting last tr and 4ch, sl st into 3rd ch of 7, sl st across 2ch.

**Round 17**: 7ch, (1tr 1 bobble into corner sp, ** 1tr in next tr, 2ch; ** repeat from ** to ** 13 times, 1 block, 2ch, 1 block, * 2ch, 1tr in next tr; * repeat from * to * 13 times, 1 bobble 1tr into corner sp, 4ch); repeat to end, omitting last tr and 4ch, sl st into 3rd ch of 7, sl st across 2ch.

**Round 18**: 7ch, (1tr 1 bobble into corner sp, ** 1tr in next tr, 2ch; ** repeat from ** to ** 6 times, 1 block, * 2ch, 1tr in next tr; * repeat from * to * 4 times, 2ch, work 2 blocks, 2ch, work 2 blocks; repeat from * to * 5 times, 2ch, 1 block; repeat from * to * 7 times, 1 bobble 1tr into corner sp, 4ch); repeat to end, omitting last tr and 4ch, sl st into 3rd ch of 7, sl st across 2ch.

**Round 19**: 7ch, (1tr 1 bobble into corner sp, ** 1tr in next tr, 2ch; ** repeat from ** to ** 6 times, 1 block, 2ch, 1 block, * 2ch, 1tr in next tr; * repeat from * to * once, 2ch, work 2 blocks, 2ch, 1 block, 2ch, 1 block, 2ch, work 2 blocks; repeat from * to * twice, 2ch, 1 block, 2ch, 1 block; repeat from * to * 7 times, 1 bobble 1tr into corner sp, 4ch); repeat to end, omitting last tr and 4ch, sl st into 3rd ch of 7, sl st across 2ch.

**Round 20**: 7ch, (1tr 1 bobble into corner sp, ** 1tr in next tr, 2ch; ** repeat from ** to ** 3 times, work 3 blocks, 2ch, 1tr in next tr, 2ch, 1 block, * 2ch, 1tr in next tr; * repeat from * to * once, 2ch, work 3 blocks, 2ch, 1 block, 2ch, 1 block, 2ch, work 3 blocks; repeat from * to * twice, 2ch, 1 block, 2ch, 1tr in next tr, 2ch, work 3 blocks; repeat from * to * 4 times, 1 bobble 1tr into corner sp, 4ch); repeat to end, omitting last tr and 4ch, sl st into 3rd ch of 7, sl st across 2ch.

**Round 21**: 7ch, (1tr 1 bobble into corner sp, ** 1tr in next tr, 2ch; ** repeat from ** to ** 3 times, 1 block, * 2ch, 1tr in next tr; * repeat from * to * once, 2ch, 1 block, 2ch, 1tr in next tr, 2ch, work 5 blocks, 2ch, 1tr in next tr, 2ch, 1 block, 2ch, 1 block, 2ch, 1tr in next tr, 2ch, work 5 blocks, 2ch, 1tr in next tr, 2ch, 1 block; repeat from * to * twice, 2ch, 1 block; repeat from * to * 4 times, 1 bobble 1tr into corner sp, 4ch); repeat to end, omitting last tr and 4ch, sl st into 3rd ch of 7, sl st across 2ch.

**Round 22**: 7ch, (1tr 1 bobble into corner sp, ** 1tr in next tr, 2ch; ** repeat from ** to ** 3 times, 1 block, * 2ch, 1tr in next tr; * repeat from * to * twice, 2ch, 1 block; repeat from * to * 3 times, 2ch, work 2 blocks; repeat from * to * twice, 2ch, 1 block, 2ch, 1 block; repeat from * to * twice, 2ch, work 2 blocks; repeat from * to * 3 times, 2ch, 1 block; repeat from * to * 3 times, 2ch, 1 block; repeat from * to * 4 times, 1 bobble 1tr into corner sp, 4ch); repeat to end, omitting last tr and 4ch, sl st into 3rd ch of 7, sl st across 2ch.

**Round 23**: 7ch, (1tr 1 bobble into corner sp, ** 1tr in next tr, 2ch; ** repeat from ** to ** 4 times, 1 block, * 2ch, 1tr in next tr; * repeat from * to * once, 2ch, 1 block; repeat from * to * 3 times, 2ch, work 2 blocks; repeat from * to * 3 times, 2ch, 1 block, 2ch, 1 block; repeat from * to * 3 times, 2ch, work 2 blocks; repeat from * to * 3 times, 2ch, 1 block; repeat from * to * twice, 2ch, 1 block; repeat from * to * 5 times, 1 bobble 1tr into corner sp, 4ch); repeat to end, omitting last tr and 4ch, sl st into 3rd ch of 7, sl st across 2ch.

**Round 24**: 7ch, (1tr 1 bobble into corner sp, ** 1tr in next tr, 2ch; ** repeat from ** to ** 5 times, work 2 blocks, * 2ch, 1tr in next tr; * repeat from * to * 3 times, 2ch, work 3 blocks; repeat from * to * 4 times, 2ch, 1 block, 2ch, 1 block; repeat from * to * 4 times, 2ch, work 3 blocks; repeat from * to * 4 times, 2ch, work 2 blocks; repeat from * to * 6 times, 1 bobble 1tr into corner sp, 4ch); repeat to end, omitting last tr and 4ch, sl st into 3rd ch of 7, sl st across 2ch.

**Round 25**: 7ch, (1 block in corner sp, 2ch, 1tr in next tr, 1 bobble in 2ch sp, 1tr in next tr, * 2ch, 1tr in next tr; * repeat from * to * 4 times, 2ch, work 8 blocks; repeat from * to * 4 times, 2ch, work 2 blocks, 2ch, work 2 blocks; repeat from * to * 4 times, 2ch, work 8 blocks; repeat from * to * 6 times, 1 bobble in 2ch sp 1tr in next tr, 2ch, 1 block in corner sp, 4ch); repeat to end, omitting last tr and 4ch, sl st into 3rd ch of 7, sl st across 2ch.

**Round 26**: 7ch, (1 block in corner sp, 2ch, 1 block, 2ch, 1tr in next tr, 1 bobble in 2ch sp, 1tr in next tr, * 2ch, 1tr in next tr; * repeat from * to * 4 times, 2ch, work 5 blocks; repeat from * to * 6 times, 2ch, work 2 blocks, 2ch, work 2 blocks; repeat from * to * 6 times, 2ch, work 5 blocks; repeat

from * to * 6 times, 1 bobble in 2ch sp, 1tr in next tr, 2ch, 1 block, 2ch, 1 block in corner sp, 4ch); repeat to end, omitting last tr and 4ch, sl st into 3rd ch of 7, sl st across 2ch.

**Round 27**: 7ch, (1 block in corner sp, * 2ch, 1tr in next tr; * repeat from * to * once, 2ch, 1 block, 2ch, 1tr in next tr, 1 bobble in 2ch sp, 1tr in next tr; repeat from * to * 13 times, 2ch, 1 block, 2ch, work 3 blocks, 2ch, work 3 blocks, 2ch, 1 block; repeat from * to * 14 times, 1 bobble in 2ch sp, 1 tr in next tr, 2ch, 1 block; repeat from * to * twice, 2ch, 1 block in corner 4ch); repeat to end, omitting last tr and 4ch, sl st into 3rd ch of 7, sl st across 2ch.

**Round 28**: 7ch, (1 block in corner sp, * 2ch, 1tr in next tr; * repeat from * to * 3 times, 2ch, 1 block, 2ch, 1tr in next tr, 1 bobble in 2ch sp, 1tr in next tr; repeat from * to * 12 times, 2ch, work 2 blocks, 2ch, work 2 blocks, 2ch, work 2 blocks, 2ch, work 2 blocks; repeat from * to * 13 times, 1 bobble in 2ch sp, 1tr in next tr, 2ch, 1 block; repeat from * to * 4 times, 2ch, 1 block in corner sp, 4ch); repeat to end, omitting last tr and 4ch, sl st into 3rd ch of 7, sl st across 2ch.

**Round 29**: 7ch, (1 block in corner sp, 2ch, 1 block, * 2ch, 1tr in next tr; * repeat from * to * once, 2ch, 1 block, 2ch, 1 block, 2ch, 1tr in next tr, 1 bobble in 2ch sp, 1tr in next tr; repeat from * to * 13 times, 2ch, work 2 blocks, 2ch, 1 block, 2ch, work 2 blocks; repeat from * to * 14 times, 1 bobble in 2ch sp, 1tr in next tr, 2ch, 1 block, 2ch, 1 block; repeat from * to * twice, 2ch, 1 block, 2ch, 1 block in corner, 4ch); repeat to end, omitting last tr and 4ch, sl st into 3rd ch of 7, sl st across 2ch.

**Round 30**: 7ch, (1 block in corner sp, * 2ch, 1tr in next tr; * repeat from * to * once, 2ch, 1 block, 2ch, 1 block; repeat from * to * twice, 2ch, 1 block 2ch, 1tr in next tr, 1 bobble in 2ch sp, 1tr in next tr; repeat from * to * 6 times, 2ch, work 2 blocks; repeat from * to * 3 times, 2ch, work 2 blocks, 2ch, 1 block, 2ch, work 2 blocks; repeat from * to * 3 times, 2ch, work 2 blocks; repeat from * to * 7 times, 1 bobble in 2ch sp, 1tr in next tr, 2ch, 1 block; repeat from * to * twice, 2ch, 1 block, 2ch ,1 block; repeat from * to * twice, 2ch, 1 block in corner sp, 4ch); repeat to end, omitting last tr and 4ch, sl st into 3rd ch of 7, sl st across 2ch.

**Round 31**: 7ch, (1 block in corner sp, * 2ch, 1tr in next tr; * repeat from * to * 3 times, 2ch, 1 block; repeat from * to * 4 times, 2ch, 1 block, 2ch, 1tr in next tr, 1 bobble in 2ch sp, 1tr in next tr; repeat from * to * 4 times, 2ch, 1 block, 2ch, 1tr in next tr, 2ch, 1 block, 2ch, 1tr in next tr, 2ch, work 2 blocks, 2ch, 1tr in next tr, 2ch, 1 block, 2ch, 1tr in next tr, 2ch, work 2 blocks, 2ch, 1tr in next tr, 2ch, 1 block, 2ch, 1tr in next tr, 2ch, 1 block; repeat from * to * 5 times, 1 bobble in 2ch sp, 1tr in next tr, 2ch, 1 block; repeat from * to * 4 times, 2ch, 1 block; repeat from * to * 4 times, 2ch, 1 block in corner sp, 4ch); repeat to end, omitting last tr and 4ch, sl st into 3rd ch of 7, sl st across 2ch.

**Round 32**: 7ch, (1 block in corner sp, ** 2ch, 1 block, 2ch, 1tr in next tr, 2ch, 1tr in next tr, 2ch, 1 block; ** repeat from ** to ** once, 2ch, 1 block, 2ch, 1tr in next tr, 1 bobble in 2ch sp, 1tr in next tr, * 2ch, 1tr in next tr; * repeat from * to * once, 2ch, 1 block; repeat from * to * twice, 2ch, 1 block, 2ch, 1tr in next tr, 2ch, work 2 blocks, 2ch, 1tr in next tr, 2ch, 1 block, 2ch, 1tr in next tr, 2ch, work 2 blocks, 2ch, 1tr in next tr, 2ch, 1 block; repeat from * to * twice, 2ch, 1 block; repeat from * to * 3 times, 1 bobble in 2ch sp, 1tr in next tr, 2ch, 1 block; repeat from ** to ** twice, 2ch, 1 block in corner sp, 4ch); repeat to end, omitting last tr and 4ch, sl st into 3rd ch of 7, sl st across 2ch.

**Round 33**: 7ch, (1 block in corner sp, ** 2ch, 1tr in next tr, 2ch, 1tr in next tr, 2ch, 1 block, 2ch, 1 block; ** repeat from ** to ** once, 2ch, 1tr in next tr, 2ch, 1tr in next tr, 2ch, 1 block, 2ch, 1tr in next tr, 1 bobble in 2ch sp, 1tr in next tr, 2ch, 1tr in next tr, 2ch, 1 block, 2ch, 1tr in next tr, 2ch, 1 block, 2ch, 1tr in next tr, 2ch, work 2 blocks, 2ch, 1tr in next tr, 2ch, work 3 blocks, 2ch, 1tr in next tr, 2ch, work 2 blocks, 2ch, 1tr in next tr, 2ch, 1 block, 2ch, 1tr in next tr, 2ch, 1 block, 2ch, 1tr in next tr, 2ch, 1tr in next tr, 1 bobble in 2ch sp, 1tr in next tr, 2ch, 1 block; repeat from ** to ** twice, 2ch, 1tr in next tr, 2ch, 1tr in next tr, 2ch, 1 block in corner sp, 4ch); repeat to end, omitting last tr and 4ch, sl st into 3rd ch of 7, sl st across 2ch.

**Round 34**: 7ch, (1 block in corner sp, ** 2ch, 1tr in next tr, 2ch, 1tr in next tr, 2ch, 1tr in next tr, 2ch, 1tr in next tr, 2ch, 1 block; ** repeat from ** to ** twice, 2ch, 1tr in next tr, 1 bobble in 2ch sp, 1tr in next tr, 2ch, 1tr in next tr, 2ch, 1 block, 2ch, 1tr in next tr, 2ch, 1tr in next tr, 2ch, work 2 blocks, 2ch, 1tr in next tr, 2ch, 1tr in next tr, 2ch, work 3 blocks, 2ch, 1tr in next tr, 2ch, 1tr in next tr, 2ch, work 2 blocks, 2ch, 1tr in next tr, 2ch, 1tr in next tr, 2ch, 1 block, 2ch, 1tr in next tr, 2ch, 1tr in next tr, 1 bobble in 2ch sp, 1tr in next tr, 2ch, 1 block; repeat from ** to ** 3 times, 4ch); repeat to end, omitting last tr and 4ch, sl st into 3rd ch of 7, sl st across 2ch.

**Round 35**: 7ch, (1 block in corner sp, ** 2ch, 1 block, 2ch, 1tr in next tr, 2ch, 1tr in next tr, 2ch, 1 block; ** repeat from ** to ** twice, 2ch, 1 block, 2ch, 1tr in next tr, 1 bobble in 2ch sp, 1tr in next tr, 2ch, 1tr in next tr, 2ch, work 3 blocks, * 2ch, 1tr in next tr; * repeat from * to * 3 times, 2ch, work 3 blocks; repeat from * to * 4 times, 2ch, work 3 blocks, 2ch, 1tr in next tr, 2ch, 1tr in next tr, 1 bobble in 2ch sp, 1tr in next tr, 2ch, 1 block; repeat from ** to ** 3 times, 2ch, 1 block in corner sp, 4ch); repeat to end, omitting last tr and 4ch, sl st into 3rd ch of 7, sl st across 2ch.

**Round 36**: 7ch, (1 block in corner sp, ** 2ch, 1tr in next tr, 2ch, 1tr in next tr, 2ch, 1 block, 2ch, 1 block; ** repeat from ** to ** twice, 2ch, 1tr in next tr, 2ch, 1tr in next tr, 2ch, 1 block, 2ch, 1tr in next tr, 1 bobble in 2ch sp, 1tr in next tr, * 2ch, 1tr in next tr; * repeat from * to * 7 times, 2ch, work 3 blocks; repeat from * to * 9 times, 1 bobble in 2ch sp, 1tr in next tr, 2ch, 1 block; repeat from ** to ** 3 times, 2ch, 1tr in next tr, 2ch, 1tr in next tr, 2ch, 1 block in corner sp, 4ch); repeat to end, omitting last tr and 4ch, sl st into 3rd ch of 7, sl st across 2ch.

**Round 37**: 7ch, (1 block in corner sp, ** 2ch, 1tr in next tr, 2ch, 1tr in next tr, 2ch, 1tr in next tr, 2ch, 1tr in next tr, 2ch, 1 block; ** repeat from ** to ** 3 times, 2ch, 1tr in next tr, 1 bobble in 2ch sp, 1tr in next tr, * 2ch, 1tr in next tr; * repeat from * to * 6 times, 2ch, work 3 blocks; repeat from * to * 8 times, 1 bobble in 2ch sp, 1tr in next tr, 2ch, 1 block; repeat from ** to ** 4 times, 4ch); repeat to end, omitting last tr and 4ch, sl st into 3rd ch of 7, sl st across 2ch.

**Round 38**: 7ch, (1 block in corner sp, ** 2ch, 1 block, 2ch, 1tr in next tr, 2ch, 1tr in next tr, 2ch, 1 block; ** repeat from ** to ** 3 times, 2ch, 1 block, 2ch, 1tr in next tr, 1 bobble in 2ch sp, 1tr in next tr, * 2ch, 1tr in next tr; * repeat from * to * 6 times, 2ch, 1 block; repeat from * to * 8 times, 1 bobble in 2ch sp, 1tr in next tr, 2ch, 1 block; repeat from ** to ** 4 times, 2ch, 1 block in corner sp, 4ch); repeat to end, omitting last tr and 4ch, sl st into 3rd ch of 7, sl st across 2ch.

**Round 39**: 7ch, (1 block in corner sp, ** 2ch, 1tr in next tr, 2ch, 1tr in next tr, 2ch, 1 block, 2ch, 1 block; ** repeat from ** to ** 3 times, 2ch, 1tr in next tr, 2ch, 1tr in next tr, 2ch, 1 block, 2ch, 1tr in next tr, 1 bobble in 2ch sp, 1tr in next tr, * 2ch, 1tr in next tr; * repeat from * to * 14 times, 1 bobble in 2ch sp, 1tr in next tr, 2ch, 1 block; repeat from ** to ** 4 times, 2ch, 1tr in next tr, 2ch, 1tr in next tr, 2ch, 1 block in corner sp, 4ch); repeat to end, omitting last tr and 4ch, sl st into 3rd ch of 7, sl st across 2ch.

**Round 40**: 7ch, (1 block in corner sp, ** 2ch, 1tr in next tr, 2ch, 1tr in next tr, 2ch, 1tr in next tr, 2ch, 1tr in next tr, 2ch, 1 block; ** repeat from ** to ** 4 times, 2ch, 1tr in next tr, 1 bobble in 2ch sp, 1tr in next tr, * 2ch, 1tr in next tr; * repeat from * to * 12 times, 1 bobble in 2ch sp, 1tr in next tr, 2ch, 1 block; repeat from ** to ** 5 times, 4ch); repeat to end, omitting last tr and 4ch, sl st into 3rd ch of 7, sl st across 2ch.

**Round 41**: 7ch, (1 block in corner sp, ** 2ch, 1 block, 2ch, 1tr in next tr, 2ch, 1tr in next tr, 2ch, 1 block; ** repeat from ** to ** 4 times, 2ch, 1 block, 2ch, 1tr in next tr, 1 bobble in 2ch sp, 1tr in next tr, * 2ch, 1tr in next tr; * repeat from * to * 10 times, 1 bobble in 2ch sp, 1tr in next tr, 2ch, 1 block; repeat from ** to ** 5 times, 2ch, 1 block in corner sp, 4ch); repeat to end, omitting last tr and 4ch, sl st into 3rd ch of 7, sl st across 2ch.

**Round 42**: 7ch, (1 block in corner sp, ** 2ch, 1tr in next tr, 2ch, 1tr in next tr, 2ch, 1 block, 2ch, 1 block; ** repeat from ** to ** 4 times, 2ch, 1tr in next tr, 2ch, 1tr in next tr, 2ch, 1 block, 2ch, 1tr in next tr, 1 bobble in 2ch sp, 1tr in next tr, * 2ch, 1tr in next tr; * repeat from * to * 8 times, 1 bobble in 2ch sp, 1tr in next tr, 2ch, 1 block; repeat from ** to ** 5 times, 2ch, 1tr in next tr, 2ch, 1tr in next tr, 2ch, 1 block in corner sp, 4ch); repeat to end, omitting last tr and 4ch, sl st into 3rd ch of 7, sl st across 2ch.

**Round 43**: 7ch, (1 block in corner sp, ** 2ch, 1tr in next tr, 2ch, 1tr in next tr, 2ch, 1tr in next tr, 2ch, 1tr in next tr, 2ch, 1 block; ** repeat from ** to ** 5 times, 2ch, 1tr in next tr, 1 bobble in 2ch sp, 1tr in next tr, * 2ch, 1tr in next tr; * repeat from * to * 6 times, 1 bobble in 2ch sp, 1tr in next tr, 2ch, 1 block; repeat from ** to ** 6 times, 4ch); repeat to end, omitting last tr and 4ch, sl st into 3rd ch of 7, sl st across 2ch.

**Round 44:** 7ch, (1 block in corner sp, ** 2ch, 1 block, 2ch, 1tr in next tr, 2ch, 1tr in next tr, 2ch, 1 block; ** repeat from ** to ** 5 times, 2ch, 1 block, 2ch, 1tr in next tr, 1 bobble in 2ch sp, 1tr in next tr, * 2ch, 1tr in next tr; * repeat from * to * 4 times, 1 bobble in 2ch sp, 1tr in next tr, 2ch, 1 block; repeat from ** to ** 6 times, 2ch, 1 block in corner sp, 4ch); repeat to end, omitting last tr and 4ch, sl st into 3rd ch of 7, sl st across 2ch.

**Round 45:** 7ch, (1 block in corner sp, ** 2ch, 1tr in next tr, 2ch, 1tr in next tr, 2ch, 1 block, 2ch, 1 block; ** repeat from ** to ** 5 times, 2ch, 1tr in next tr, 2ch, 1tr in next tr, 2ch, 1 block, 2ch, 1tr in next tr, 1 bobble in 2ch sp, 1tr in next tr, * 2ch, 1tr in next tr; * repeat from * to * twice, 1 bobble in 2ch sp, 1tr in next tr, 2ch, 1 block; repeat from ** to ** 6 times, 2ch, 1tr in next tr, 2ch, 1tr in next tr, 2ch, 1 block in corner sp, 4ch); repeat to end, omitting last tr and 4ch, sl st into 3rd ch of 7, sl st across 2ch.

**Round 46:** 7ch, (1 block in corner sp, ** 2ch, 1tr in next tr, 2ch, 1tr in next tr, 2ch, 1tr in next tr, 2ch, 1tr in next tr, 2ch, 1 block; ** repeat from ** to ** 6 times, 2ch, 1tr in next tr, 1 bobble in 2ch sp, 1tr in next tr, 2ch, 1tr in next tr, 1 bobble in 2ch sp, 1tr in next tr, 2ch, 1 block; repeat from ** to ** 7 times, 4ch); repeat to end, omitting last tr and 4ch, sl st into 3rd ch of 7, sl st across 2ch.

**Round 47:** 7ch, (1 block in corner sp, ** 2ch, 1 block, 2ch, 1tr in next tr, 2ch, 1tr in next tr, 2ch, 1 block; ** repeat from ** to ** 6 times, 2ch, 1 block, 2ch, 1tr in next tr, 1 bobble in 2ch sp, 1tr in next tr, 2ch, 1 block; repeat from ** to ** 7 times, 2ch, 1 block in corner sp, 4ch); repeat to end, omitting last tr and 4ch, sl st into 3rd ch of 7, sl st across 2ch.

**Round 48:** 7ch, (1 block in corner sp, ** 2ch, 1tr in next tr, 2ch, 1tr in next tr, 2ch, 1 block, 2ch, 1 block; ** repeat from ** to ** 14 times, 2ch, 1tr in next tr, 2ch, 1tr in next tr, 2ch, 1 block in corner sp, 4ch); repeat to end, omitting last tr and 4ch, sl st into 3rd ch of 7, sl st across 2ch.

**Round 49:** 7ch, (1 block in corner sp, ** 2ch, 1tr in next tr, 2ch, 1tr in next tr, 2ch, 1tr in next tr, 2ch, 1tr in next tr, 2ch, 1 block; ** repeat from ** to ** 15 times, 4ch); repeat to end, omitting last tr and 4ch, sl st into 3rd ch of 7, sl st across 2ch.

**Round 50:** 7ch, (1tr 1 bobble into corner sp, 5ch, sl st into first ch [picot worked], 1tr into first tr of next block, 2ch, 1tr into 3rd tr of same block, 1 bobble in 2ch sp, 1 picot, 1tr in next tr; repeat * 2ch, miss 2ch sp, 1tr in next tr, 1 bobble in 2ch sp, 1 picot, 1tr in next tr, * to corner, at corner work 1tr into 3rd tr of same block, 1 bobble into corner sp, 1 picot, 1tr into corner, 4ch); repeat to end, omitting last tr and 4ch, sl st into 3rd ch of 7, and fasten off.

Make the first square 50 rounds; work second square to 49 rounds and join to first square like this; work as for round 50, joining the squares together with the picots, second square picots are worked. Ch3, sl st into picot of first square, 2ch, then sl st into the first ch of 3, work same for squares 3 and 4.

For outer edging repeat round 50 around all four joined squares.

# Courtelle
# baby blanket
# and blocks

*You can use any leftover wool to make squares for the baby blocks, which are a great idea for a gift for a new mother, or a mother-to-be.*

## Materials

*Baby blanket*

Courtelle 8 ply
Blue 3 × 100g balls
Yellow 3 × 100g balls
Pink 3 × 100g balls
Light green 3 × 100g balls
White 4 × 100g balls

*Blocks*

Any leftover blue, yellow, pink, light green and white courtelle
White 16 ply — 1 ball (2 strands of 8 ply together)
Four cubes of foam 12 cm x 12 cm (5 in x 5 in)

*Hook sizes*: 3.00 mm; 3.50 mm
*Tension*: 23 treble measured over the 3rd round of baby = 10 cm (4 in).

*Notes*: For the bobble, work 5tr into next st, remove hook from loop, insert hook in first treble of 5 treble group then back into loop and draw the loop through the treble, 1ch to fasten off.

For the block, work 3tr plus 2tr for each additional block in group.

Difficulty: *easy*

Work the blanket with the 3.00 mm hook. Ch8, sl st into first ch to form ring.

**Round 1**: 7ch, (3tr into ring, 4ch) 3 times; 2tr into ring, sl st into 3rd ch of 7, sl st across 2ch.

**Round 2**: 7ch, (1tr into each of next 2ch, 1tr in next tr, 1ch, miss 1tr, 1tr in next tr, 1tr into each of next 2ch, 4ch); repeat to end, sl st into 3rd ch of 7, sl st across 2ch.

**Round 3**: 7ch, (1tr in each of next 2ch, 1tr in next tr, 1ch, miss 1tr, 1tr in next tr, 1ch, 1tr in next tr, 1ch, miss 1tr, 1tr in next tr, 1tr in each of next 2ch, 4ch); repeat to end, sl st into 3rd ch of 7, sl st across 2ch.

**Round 4**: 7ch, (1tr in each of next 2ch, 1ch, miss 1tr, 1tr in next tr, * 1ch, 1tr in next tr; * repeat from * to * twice, 1ch, miss 1tr, 1 block, 4ch); repeat to end, sl st into 3rd ch of 7, sl st across 2ch.

**Round 5**: 7ch, (1tr in each of next 2ch, 1tr in next tr, 1ch, miss 1tr, 1tr in next tr, 1tr in 1ch, 1tr in next tr, 1ch, 1tr in next tr, 1ch, 1tr in next tr, 1ch, 1tr in next tr, 1tr in 1ch, 1tr in next tr, 1ch, miss 1tr, 1tr in next tr, 1tr in each of next 2ch, 4ch); repeat to end, sl st into 3rd ch of 7, sl st across 2ch.

**Round 6**: 7ch, (1 block, 1ch, miss 1tr, 1tr in next tr, 1ch, miss 1ch sp, 1tr in next tr, 1ch, miss 1tr, 1 block, 1ch, miss 1ch sp, 1 block, 1ch, miss 1tr, 1tr in next tr, 1ch, miss 1ch sp, 1tr in next tr, 1ch, miss 1tr, 1 block, 4ch); repeat to end, sl st into 3rd ch of 7, sl st across 2ch.

**Round 7**: 7ch, (1 block, 1ch, miss 1tr, 1tr in next tr, * 1ch, 1tr in next tr; * repeat from * to * twice, 1ch, miss 1tr, 1 block, 1ch, miss 1tr, 1tr in next tr; repeat from * to * 3 times, 1ch, miss 1tr, 1 block, 4ch); repeat to end, sl st into 3rd ch of 7, sl st across 2ch.

**Round 8**: 7ch, (1 block, 1ch, miss 1tr, 1tr in next tr, * 1ch, 1tr in next tr; * repeat from * to * 4 times, 1ch, miss 1 tr, 1tr in next tr; repeat from * to * 5 times, 1ch, miss 1tr, 1 block, 4ch); repeat to end, sl st into 3rd ch of 7, sl st across 2ch.

Round 9 is worked in white. **Round 9**: 7ch, (1tr 1 bobble in corner sp, 1tr in next tr, 1ch, miss 1tr, 1tr in next tr, 1 bobble in 1ch sp, 1tr in next tr, * 1ch, 1tr in next tr, 1 bobble in 1ch sp, 1tr in next tr; * repeat from * to * 5 times, 1ch, miss 1 tr, 1tr in next tr, 1 bobble 1tr in corner sp, 4ch); repeat to end, sl st into 3rd ch of 7, sl st across 2ch.

Round 10 is worked in first colour. **Round 10**: 7ch, (1 block, 1ch, miss bobble, 1tr in next tr, * 1ch, miss 1ch sp, 1tr in next tr, 1ch, miss bobble, 1tr in next tr; * repeat from * to * 6 times, 1ch, miss 1ch sp, 1tr in next tr, 1ch, 1 block, 4ch); repeat to end, sl st into 3rd ch of 7, sl st across 2ch.

**Round 11**: 7ch, (1 block, 1ch, miss 1tr, 1tr in next tr, * 1ch, 1tr in next tr; * repeat from * to * 16 times, 1ch, miss 1tr, 1 block, 4ch); repeat to end, sl st into 3rd ch of 7, sl st across 2ch.

**Round 12**: 7ch, (1 block, 1ch, miss 1tr, 1tr in next tr, 1ch, miss 1ch sp, 1 block, * 1ch, 1tr in next tr; * repeat from * to * once, 1ch, work 4 blocks in next four 1ch spaces, 1ch, miss 1ch sp, 1 block in next 1ch sp, 1ch, 1tr in next tr, 1ch, 1 block, 1ch, miss 1ch sp, 4 blocks, 1ch, miss 1tr, 1 block, 4ch); repeat to end, sl st into 3rd ch of 7, sl st across 2ch.

**Round 13**: 7ch, (1 block, 1ch, miss 1tr, 1tr in next tr, 1ch, 1tr in next tr, 1ch, 1 block, 1ch, 1tr in next tr, 1ch, 1tr in next tr, 1ch, 1 block, 1ch, miss 1tr, 1 tr in next tr, 1ch, miss 1tr, 1 block, 1ch, miss 1ch sp, 1 block, 1ch, 1tr in next tr, 1ch, 1 block, 1ch, miss 1ch sp, 1 block, 1ch, miss 1tr, 1tr in next tr, 1ch, miss 1tr, 1 block, 1ch, 1tr in next tr, 1ch, miss 1tr, 1 block, 4ch); repeat to end, sl st into 3rd ch of 7, sl st across 2ch.

**Round 14**: 7ch, (1 block, 1ch, miss 1tr, 1tr in next tr, * 1ch, 1tr in next tr; * repeat from * to * once, 1ch, 1 block; repeat from * to * 3 times, 1ch, miss 1tr, work 3 blocks, 1ch, miss 1ch sp, work 4 blocks, 1ch, 1tr in next tr, miss 1tr, work 3 blocks; repeat from * to * twice, 1ch, miss 1tr, 1 block, 4ch); repeat to end, sl st into 3rd ch of 7, sl st across 2ch.

**Round 15**: 7ch, (1 block, 1ch, miss 1tr, 1tr in next tr, * 1ch, 1tr in next tr; * repeat from * to * once, 1ch, 1 block, 1ch, miss 1tr, 1 block, 1ch, 1tr in next tr, 1ch, 1 block, 1ch, miss 1tr, 1tr in next tr, 1ch, miss 1tr, 1 block, 1ch, miss 1ch sp, 1 block, 1ch, miss 1tr, 1tr into next tr, 1ch, miss 1tr, 1 block, 1ch, miss 1ch sp, 1 block, 1ch, miss 1tr, 1tr in next tr, 1ch, miss 1tr, 1 block; repeat from * to * 3 times, 1ch, miss 1tr, 1 block, 4ch); repeat to end, sl st into 3rd ch of 7, sl st across 2ch.

**Round 16**: 7ch, (1 block, 1ch, miss 1tr, 1tr in next tr, * 1 ch, 1tr in next tr; * repeat from * to * once, 1ch, 1 block, 1ch, miss 1tr, 1tr in next tr, 1ch, miss 1ch sp, 1tr in next tr, 1 ch, miss 1tr, 1 block, 1ch, miss 1ch sp, work 4 blocks, 1ch, miss 1ch sp, work 4 blocks, 1ch, miss 1ch sp, work 4 blocks; repeat from * to * 4 times, 1ch, miss 1tr, 1 block, 4ch); repeat to end, sl st into 3rd ch of 7, sl st across 2ch.

**Round 17**: 7ch, (1 block, 1ch, miss 1tr, 1tr in next tr, * 1ch, 1tr in next tr; * repeat from * to * 3 times, 1ch, miss 1tr, 1tr in next tr; repeat from * to * 3 times, 1ch, miss 1tr, 1tr in next tr, 1 ch, miss 1ch sp, 1tr in next tr, ** 1ch, miss 1tr, 1tr in next tr; ** repeat from ** to ** 13 times; repeat from * to * 5 times, 1ch, miss 1tr, 1 block, 4ch); repeat to end, sl st into 3rd ch of 7, sl st across 2ch.

**Round 18**: 7ch, (1 block, 1ch, miss 1tr, 1tr in next tr, * 1ch, 1tr in next tr; * repeat from * to * 30 times, 1ch, miss 1tr, 1 block, 4ch); repeat to end, sl st into 3rd ch of 7, sl st across 2ch.

**Round 19** is worked in white. Ch7, (1tr in each of next 2ch, 1tr in each of next 3tr, 1tr in each tr and ch to corner, work 1tr in each of next 2ch, 4ch), 75 treble in all; repeat to end, sl st into 3rd ch of 7. Fasten off.

Work 16 squares in all: that is, four pink and white; four blue and white; four light green and white; four yellow and white. With right sides together sew tr to tr to give a neat finish.

For the edging work 7ch in a corner sp, work 1tr in every tr and ch to corner, 4ch; repeat to end, sl st into 3rd ch of 7. Work one more round in this manner.

To finish, press work on the wrong side with a damp cloth and a warm iron, taking care not to flatten bobbles.

## To make the baby blocks

Work the blocks with the 3.00 mm hook. Ch8, sl st into first ch to form ring.

**Round 1**: 7ch, (3tr into ring, 4ch) 3 times; 2tr into ring, sl st into 3rd ch of 7, this makes 3rd tr, sl st across 2ch.

**Round 2**: 7ch, (1tr into each of next 2ch, 1tr in each of next 3tr, 1tr in each of next 2ch, [7 trebles worked] 4ch); repeat to end, sl st into 3rd ch of 7, sl st across 2ch.

**Round 3**: 7ch, (1tr in each of next 2ch, 1tr in each of next 7tr, 1tr in each of next 2ch, [11 trebles worked] 4ch); repeat to end, sl st into 3rd ch of 7, sl st across 2ch.

**Round 4**: 7ch, (1tr in each of next 2ch, 1tr in each of next 11tr, 1tr in each of next 2ch, [15 trebles worked] 4ch); repeat to end, sl st into 3rd ch of 7, sl st across 2ch.

**Round 5**: 7ch, (1tr in each of next 2ch, 1tr in each of next 15tr, 1tr in each of next 2ch, [19 trebles worked] 4ch); repeat to end, sl st into 3rd ch of 7. Fasten off.

You will need to make 6 squares of the same colour. Join 2 strands of white yarn together (16 ply) and change to 3.50 mm hook.

To make the letters A, B, C, D, you will need to make:

A = 29ch + 10ch for piece that goes across the middle of the A
B = 65ch
C = 41ch
D = 50ch

For the numbers 1, 2, 3, 4, you will need to make:

1 = 17ch
2 = 45ch
3 = 52ch
4 = 48ch

Sew numbers and letters on squares before joining together.

You will need four foam blocks for the blocks, plus some white fabric to cover the foam. Put it all together and you have a wonderful gift!

| YELLOW | BLUE | PINK | LIME |
|--------|------|------|------|
| PINK | LIME | YELLOW | BLUE |
| BLUE | PINK | LIME | YELLOW |
| LIME | YELLOW | BLUE | PINK |

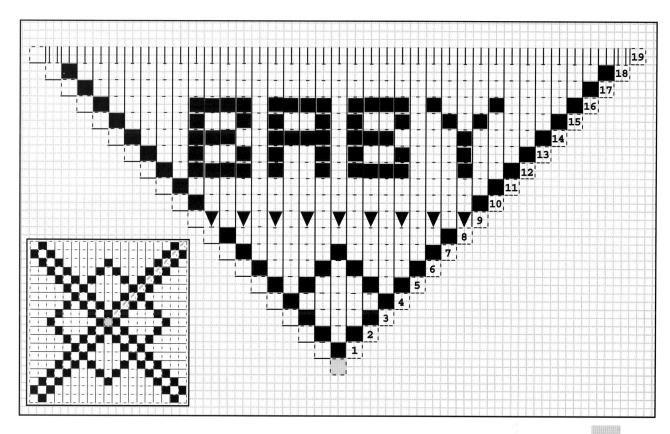

# Six-square
# pram cover

*I've never been able to find a really good pattern for a pram cover that I was satisfied with, so I decided to design my own. The result is this lovely filet and bobble crochet pram cover made from pure baby wool.*

## Materials

Pure wool 4 ply
Cream 36 × 25g balls

*Hook size*: 1.75 mm
*Tension*: 36 trebles to 10 cm (4 in) on flat work.

*Note*: For the bobble, work 5tr into next st, remove hook from loop, insert hook in first tr of 5tr group then back into loop and draw the loop through the tr, 1ch to fasten off.

Difficulty: *hard*

Ch8, sl st into first ch to form ring.

**Round 1**: 7ch, (1tr 1 bobble 1tr into ring, 4ch) 3 times; 1tr 1 bobble into ring, sl st into 3rd ch of 7, this makes the last tr, sl st across 2ch.

**Round 2**: 7ch, (1tr 1 bobble into corner sp, 1tr into next tr, 2ch, 1tr into next tr, 1 bobble 1tr into corner sp, 4ch); repeat to end, omitting last tr, sl st into 3rd ch of 7, sl st across 2ch.

**Round 3**: 7ch, (1tr 1 bobble into corner sp, 1tr into next tr, 2ch, 1tr into next tr, 2ch, 1tr into next tr, 2ch, 1tr into next tr, 1 bobble 1tr into corner sp, 4ch); repeat to end, omitting last tr in corner sp, sl st into 3rd ch of 7, sl st across 2ch.

**Round 4**: 7ch, (1tr 1 bobble into corner sp, 1tr into next tr, 2ch, 1tr in next tr, 2ch, 1tr in next tr, 2ch, 1tr in next tr, 2ch, 1tr in next tr, 2ch, 1tr in next tr, 1 bobble 1tr into corner sp, 4ch); repeat to end, omitting last tr in corner sp, sl st into 3rd ch of 7, sl st across 2ch.

**Round 5**: 7ch, (1tr 1 bobble into corner sp, 1tr into next tr, * 2ch, 1tr in next tr; * repeat from * to * 6 times, 1 bobble 1tr into corner sp, 4ch); repeat to end, omitting last tr in corner sp, sl st into 3rd ch of 7, sl st across 2ch.

**Round 6**: 7ch, (1tr 1 bobble into corner sp, 1tr in next tr, * 2ch, 1tr in next tr; * repeat from * to * 8 times, 1 bobble 1tr into corner sp, 4ch); repeat to end, omitting last tr, sl st into 3rd ch of 7, sl st across 2ch.

**Round 7**: 7ch, (1tr 1 bobble into corner sp, 1tr in next tr, * 2ch, 1tr in next tr; * repeat from * to * 4 times, 1 bobble in 2ch sp, 1tr in next tr; repeat from * to * 5 times, 1 bobble 1tr into corner sp, 4ch); repeat to end, omitting last tr, sl st into 3rd ch of 7, sl st across 2ch.

**Round 8**: 7ch, (1tr 1 bobble into corner sp, 1tr in next tr, * 2ch, 1tr in next tr; * repeat from * to * 4 times, 1 bobble in 2ch sp, 1tr in next tr, 2ch, 1tr in next tr, 1 bobble into 2ch sp, 1tr in next tr; repeat from * to * 5 times, 1 bobble 1tr into corner sp, 4ch); repeat to end, omitting last tr in corner sp, sl st into 3rd ch of 7, sl st across 2ch.

**Round 9**: 7ch, (1tr 1 bobble into corner sp, 1tr in next tr, * 2ch, 1tr in next tr; * repeat from * to * 4 times, 1 bobble into 2ch sp, 1tr in next tr, 2ch, 1tr in next tr, 1tr in 1ch, miss 1ch, 1tr in next tr, 2ch, 1tr in next tr, 1 bobble in 2ch sp, 1tr in next tr; repeat from * to * 5 times, 1 bobble 1tr into corner sp, 4ch); repeat to end, omitting last tr in corner sp, sl st into 3rd ch of 7, sl st across 2ch.

**Round 10**: 7ch, (1tr 1 bobble into corner sp, 1tr in next tr, * 2ch, 1tr in next tr; * repeat from * to * 4 times, 1 bobble in 2ch sp, 1tr in next tr, 2ch, 1tr in next tr, 1tr in 1ch, miss 1ch, 1tr in each of next 3tr, 1tr in 1ch, miss 1ch, 1tr in next tr, 2ch, 1tr in next tr, 1 bobble in 2ch sp, 1tr in next tr; repeat from * to * 5 times, 1 bobble 1tr in corner sp, 4ch); repeat to end, omitting last tr, sl st into 3rd ch of 7, sl st across 2ch.

**Round 11**: 7ch, (1tr 1 bobble in corner sp, 1tr in next tr, * 2ch, 1tr in next tr; * repeat from * to * 4 times, 1 bobble in 2ch sp, 1tr in next tr, 2ch, 1tr in next tr, 1tr in 1ch, miss 1ch, 1tr in each of next 7tr, 1tr in 1ch, miss 1ch, 1tr in next tr, 2ch, 1tr in next tr, 1 bobble in 2ch sp, 1tr in next tr; repeat from * to * 5 times, 1 bobble 1tr in corner sp, 4ch); repeat to end, omitting last tr, sl st into 3rd ch of 7, sl st across 2ch.

**Round 12**: 7ch, (1tr 1 bobble in corner sp, 1tr in next tr, * 2ch, 1tr in next tr; * repeat from * to * 4 times, 1 bobble in 2ch sp, 1tr in next tr, 2ch, 1tr in next tr, 1tr in 1ch, miss 1ch, 1tr in each of next 11tr, 1tr in 1ch, miss 1ch, 1tr in next tr, 2ch, 1tr in next tr, 1 bobble in 2ch sp, 1tr in next tr; repeat from *

to * 5 times, 1 bobble 1tr in corner sp, 4ch); repeat to end, omitting last tr, sl st into 3rd ch of 7, sl st across 2ch.

**Round 13**: 7ch, (1tr 1 bobble into corner sp, 1tr in next tr, * 2ch, 1tr in next tr; * repeat from * to * 4 times, 1 bobble in 2ch sp, 1tr in next tr, 2ch, 1tr in next tr, 1tr in 1ch, miss 1ch, 1tr in each of next 6tr, 3ch, miss 3tr, 1tr in each of next 6tr, 1tr in 1ch, miss 1ch, 1tr in next tr, 2ch, 1tr in next tr, 1 bobble in 2ch sp, 1tr in next tr; repeat from * to * 5 times, 1 bobble 1tr in corner sp, 4ch); repeat to end, omitting last tr in corner sp, sl st into 3rd ch of 7, sl st across 2ch.

**Round 14**: 7ch, (1tr 1 bobble in corner sp, 1tr in next tr, * 2ch, 1tr in next tr; * repeat from * to * 4 times, 1 bobble in 2ch sp, 1tr in next tr, 2ch, 1tr in next tr, 1tr in 1ch, miss 1ch, 1tr in each of next 4tr, 3ch, miss 3tr, 1tr in next tr, 3ch, 1dc in middle ch of next 3ch, 3ch, 1tr in next tr, 3ch, miss 3tr, 1tr in each of next 4tr, 1tr in 1ch, miss 1ch, 1tr in next tr, 2ch, 1tr in next tr, 1 bobble in 2ch sp, 1tr in next tr; repeat from * to * 5 times, 1 bobble 1tr in corner sp, 4ch); repeat to end, omitting last tr, sl st into 3rd ch of 7, sl st across 2ch.

**Round 15**: 7ch, (1tr in each of next 2ch, 1tr in next tr, 2ch, 1tr in next tr, 1 bobble in 2ch sp, 1tr in next

tr, * 2ch, 1tr in next tr; * repeat from * to * 4 times, 1 bobble in 2ch sp, 1tr in next tr, 2ch, miss 1tr, 1tr in each of next 4tr, 1tr in each of next 3ch, 1tr in next tr, 3ch, 1tr in next tr, 1tr in each of next 3ch, 1tr in each of next 4tr, 2ch, miss 1tr, 1tr in next tr, 1 bobble in 2ch sp, 1tr in next tr; repeat from * to * 5 times, 1 bobble in 2ch sp, 1tr in next tr, 2ch, 1tr in next tr, 1tr in each of next 2ch, 4ch); repeat to end, omitting last tr in ch, work a sl st into 3rd ch of 7, sl st across 2ch.

**Round 16**: 7ch, (1tr in each of next 2ch, 1tr in each of next 3tr, 1tr in 1ch, miss 1ch, 1tr in next tr, [7 treble in all], 2ch, 1tr in next tr, 1 bobble in 2ch sp, 1tr in next tr, * 2ch, 1tr in next tr; * repeat from * to * 4 times, 1 bobble in 2ch sp, 1tr in next tr, 2ch, miss 1tr, 1tr in each of next 6tr, 1tr in each of next 3ch, 1tr in each of next 6tr, 2ch, miss 1tr, 1tr in next tr, 1 bobble in 2ch sp, 1tr in next tr; repeat from * to * 5 times, 1 bobble in 2ch sp, 1tr in next tr, 2ch, 1tr in next tr, 1tr in 1ch, miss 1ch, 1tr in each of next 3tr, 1tr in each of next 2ch, 4ch); repeat to end, omitting last tr in ch, sl st into 3rd ch of 7, sl st across 2ch.

**Round 17**: 7ch, (1tr in each of next 2ch, 1tr in each of next 7tr, 1tr in 1ch, miss 1ch, 1tr in next tr, [11 treble in all], 2ch, 1tr in next tr, 1 bobble in 2ch sp, 1tr in next tr, * 2ch, 1tr in next tr; * repeat from

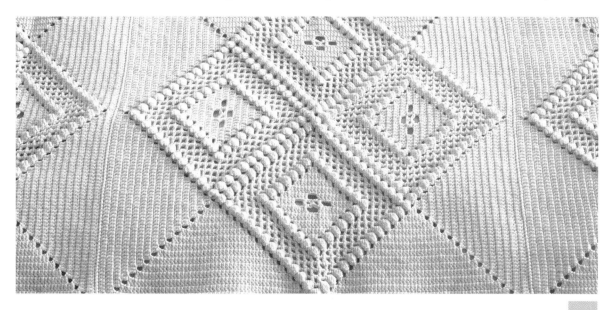

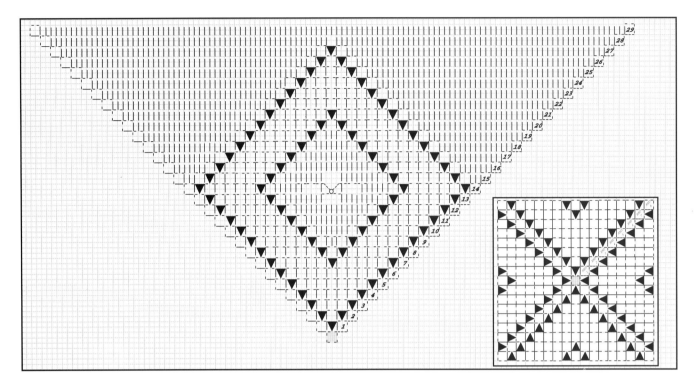

* to * 4 times, 1 bobble in 2ch sp, 1tr in next tr, 2ch, miss 1tr, 1tr in each of next 11tr, miss 1tr, 2ch, 1tr in next tr, 1 bobble in 2ch sp, 1tr in next tr; repeat from * to * 5 times, 1 bobble in 2ch sp, 1tr in next tr, 2ch, 1tr in next tr, 1tr in 1ch, miss 1ch, 1tr in each of next 7tr, 1tr in each of next 2ch, [11 treble] 4ch); repeat to end, omitting last tr in ch, sl st into 3rd ch of 7, sl st across 2ch.

**Round 18**: 7ch, (1tr in each of next 2ch, 1tr in each of next 11tr, 1tr in 1ch, miss 1ch, 1tr in next tr, 2ch, 1tr in next tr, 1 bobble in 2ch sp, 1tr in next tr, * 2ch, 1tr in next tr; * repeat from * to * 4 times, 1 bobble in 2ch sp, 1tr in next tr, 2ch, miss 1tr, 1tr in each of next 7tr, miss 1tr, 2ch, 1tr in next tr, 1 bobble in 2ch sp, 1tr in next tr; repeat from * to * 5 times, 1 bobble in 2ch sp, 1tr in next tr, 2ch, 1tr in next tr, 1tr in 1ch, miss 1ch, 1tr in each of next 11tr, 1tr in each of next 2ch, 4ch); repeat to end, omitting last tr in ch, sl st into 3rd ch of 7, sl st across 2ch.

**Round 19**: 7ch, (1tr in each of next 2ch, 1tr in each of next 15tr, 1tr in 1ch, miss 1ch, 1tr in next tr, 2ch, 1tr in next tr, 1 bobble in 2ch sp, 1tr in next

tr, * 2ch, 1tr in next tr; * repeat from * to * 4 times, 1 bobble in 2ch sp, 1tr in next tr, 2ch, miss 1tr, 1tr in each of next 3tr, 2ch, miss 1tr, 1tr in next tr, 1 bobble in 2ch sp, 1tr in next tr; repeat from * to * 5 times, 1 bobble in 2ch sp, 1tr in next tr, 2ch, 1tr in next tr, 1tr in 1ch, miss 1ch, 1tr in each of next 15tr, 1tr in each of next 2ch, 4ch); repeat to end, omitting last tr in ch, sl st into 3rd ch of 7, sl st across 2ch.

**Round 20**: 7ch, (1tr in each of next 2ch, 1tr in each of next 19tr, 1tr in 1ch, miss 1ch, 1tr in next tr, 2ch, 1tr in next tr, 1 bobble in 2ch sp, 1tr in next tr, * 2ch, 1tr in next tr; * repeat from * to * 4 times, 1 bobble in 2ch sp, 1tr in next tr, 2ch, miss 1tr, 1tr in next tr, 1 bobble in 2ch sp, 1tr in next tr; repeat from * to * 5 times, 1 bobble in 2ch sp, 1 tr in next tr, 2ch, 1tr in next tr, 1tr in 1ch, miss 1ch, 1tr in each of next 19tr, 1tr in each of next 2ch, 4ch); repeat to end, omitting last tr in ch, sl st into 3rd ch of 7, sl st across 2ch.

**Round 21**: 7ch, (1tr in each of next 2ch, 1tr in each of next 23tr, 1tr in 1ch, miss 1ch, 1tr in next tr, 2ch, 1tr in next tr, 1 bobble in 2ch sp, 1tr in next tr, *

2ch, 1tr in next tr; * repeat from * to * 4 times, 1 bobble in 2ch sp, 1tr in next tr; repeat from * to * 5 times, 1 bobble in 2ch sp, 1tr in next tr, 2ch, 1tr in next tr, 1tr in 1ch, miss 1ch, 1tr in each of next 23tr, 1tr in each of next 2ch, 4ch); repeat to end, omitting last tr in ch, sl st into 3rd ch of 7, sl st across 2ch.

**Round 22**: 7ch, (1 tr in each of next 2ch, 1tr in each of next 27tr, 1tr in 1ch, miss 1ch, 1tr in next tr, 2ch, 1tr in next tr, 1 bobble in 2ch sp, 1tr in next tr, * 2ch, 1tr in next tr; * repeat from * to * 8 times, 1 bobble in 2ch sp, 1tr in next tr, 2ch, 1tr in next tr, 1tr in 1ch, miss 1ch, 1tr in each of next 27tr, 1tr in each of next 2ch, 4ch); repeat to end, omitting last tr in ch, sl st into 3rd ch of 7, sl st across 2ch.

**Round 23**: 7ch, (1tr in each of next 2ch, 1tr in each of next 31tr, 1tr in 1ch, miss 1ch, 1tr in next tr, 2ch, 1tr in next tr, 1 bobble in 2ch sp, 1tr in next tr, * 2ch, 1tr in next tr; * repeat from * to * 6 times, 1 bobble in 2ch sp, 1tr in next tr, 2ch, 1tr in next tr, 1tr in 1ch, miss 1ch, 1tr in each of next 31tr, 1tr in each of next 2ch, 4ch); repeat to end, omitting last tr in ch, sl st into 3rd ch of 7, sl st across 2ch.

**Round 24**: 7ch, (1tr in each of next 2ch, 1tr into each of next 35tr, 1tr in 1ch, miss 1ch, 1tr in next tr, 2ch, 1tr in next tr, 1 bobble in 2ch sp, 1tr in next tr, * 2ch, 1tr in next tr; * repeat from * to * 4 times, 1 bobble in 2ch sp, 1tr in next tr, 2ch, 1tr in next tr, 1tr in 1ch, miss 1ch, 1tr in each of next 35tr, 1tr in each of next 2ch, 4ch); repeat to end, omitting last tr in ch, sl st into 3rd ch of 7, sl st across 2ch.

**Round 25**: 7ch, (1tr in each of next 2ch, 1tr in each of next 39tr, 1tr in 1ch, miss 1ch, 1tr in next tr, 2ch, 1tr in next tr, 1 bobble in 2ch sp, 1tr in next tr, * 2ch, 1tr in next tr; * repeat from * to * twice, 1 bobble in 2ch sp, 1tr in next tr, 2ch, 1tr in next tr, 1tr in 1ch, miss 1ch, 1tr in each of next 39tr, 1tr in each of next 2ch, 4ch); repeat to end, omitting last tr in ch, sl st into 3rd ch of 7, sl st across 2ch.

**Round 26**: 7ch, (1tr in each of next 2ch, 1tr in each of next 43tr, 1tr in 1ch, miss 1ch, 1tr in next tr, 2ch, 1tr in next tr, 1 bobble in 2ch sp, 1tr in next tr, 2ch, 1tr in next tr, 1 bobble in 2ch sp, 1tr in next tr, 2ch, 1tr in next tr, 1tr in 1ch, miss 1ch, 1tr in each of next 43tr, 1tr in each of next 2ch, 4ch); repeat to end, omitting last tr in ch, sl st into 3rd ch of 7, sl st across 2ch.

**Round 27**: 7ch, (1tr in each of next 2ch, 1tr in each of next 47tr, 1tr in 1ch, miss 1ch, 1tr in next tr, 2ch, 1tr in next tr, 1 bobble in 2ch sp, 1tr in next tr, 2ch, 1tr in next tr, 1tr in 1ch, miss 1ch, 1tr in each of next 47tr, 1tr in each of next 2ch, 4ch); repeat to end, omitting last tr in ch, sl st into 3rd ch of 7, sl st across 2ch.

**Round 28**: 7ch, (1tr in each of next 2ch, 1tr in each of next 51tr, 1tr in 1ch, miss 1ch, 1tr in next tr, 2ch, 1tr in next tr, 1tr in 1ch, miss 1ch, 1tr in each of next 51tr, 1tr in each of next 2ch, 4ch); repeat to end, omitting last tr in ch, sl st into 3rd ch of 7, sl st across 2ch.

**Round 29**: 7ch, (1tr in each of next 2ch, 1tr in each of next 55tr, 1tr in 1ch, miss 1ch, 1tr in each of next 55tr, 1tr in each of next 2ch, 4ch); repeat to end, omitting last tr in ch, sl st into 3rd ch of 7. Fasten off.

To join squares, with right sides together sew stitch to stitch to give a neat finish. Repeat for reverse side.

For bobble edging join wool in a corner sp, work 1ch and work a dc in the same place, 4ch, work a bobble into dc, dc in same corner sp, 4ch, work a bobble into dc, (2 bobbles in corner sp), work a dc in next tr, work a bobble into dc, (1dc into 3rd tr from hook, 4ch, 1 bobble into dc); repeat to corner. Work all the way around all six squares and sl st into 1ch at the start of the round.

# White dove
# baby shawl

*This White Dove shawl has the symbol of love and peace. Nothing could be more*

*appropriate for a baby. This is made from the finest and softest baby wool.*

## Materials

Pure wool 4 ply
White 36 × 25g balls

*Hook size*: 1.75 mm
*Tension*: 36 stitches to 10 cm (4 in)
Block is (3tr to 1 block) plus 2tr for each additional block in group.
On the graph a shell is represented by a triangle. Work a shell as follows: 3tr 2ch 3tr into next space.

Difficulty: *hard*

Ch8, sl st into first ch to form ring.

**Round 1**: 7ch, (1 block in ring, 4ch); 3 times, 2tr into ring, sl st into 3rd ch of 7, this counts as a tr, sl st across 2ch.

**Round 2**: 7ch, (1tr in each of next 2ch, 1tr in next tr, 2ch, miss 1tr, 1tr in next tr, 1 tr in each of next 2ch, 4ch); repeat to end, sl st into 3rd ch of 7.

**Round 3**: 7ch, (1tr in each of next 2ch, 1tr in next tr, 2ch, miss 1tr, 1tr in next tr, 2ch, 1tr in next tr, 2ch, miss 1tr, 1tr in next tr, 1tr in each of next 2ch, 4ch); repeat to end, sl st into 3rd ch of 7, sl st across 2ch.

**Round 4**: 7ch, (1tr in each of next 2ch, 1tr in next tr, 2ch, miss 1tr, 1tr in next tr; * 2ch, 1tr in next tr; * repeat from * to * twice, 2ch, miss 1tr, 1tr in next tr, 1tr in each of next 2ch, 4ch); repeat to end, sl st into 3rd ch of 7, sl st across 2ch.

**Round 5**: 7ch, (1tr in each of next 2ch, 1tr in next tr, 2ch, miss 1tr, 1tr in next tr, 1tr in 1ch, miss 1ch, 1tr in next tr, 2ch, 1tr in next tr, 2ch, 1tr in next tr, 2ch, 1tr in next tr, 1tr in 1ch, miss 1ch, 1tr in next tr, 2ch, miss 1tr, 1tr in next tr, 1tr in each of next 2ch, 4ch); repeat to end, sl st into 3rd ch of 7, sl st across 2ch.

**Round 6**: 7ch, (1tr in each of next 2ch, 1tr in next tr, 2ch, miss 1tr, 1tr in next tr, 2ch, 1tr in next tr, 2ch, miss 1tr, 1tr in next tr, 1tr in 1ch, miss 1ch, 1tr in next tr, 2ch, 1tr in next tr, 1tr in 1ch, miss 1ch, 1tr in next tr, 2ch, miss 1tr, 1tr in next tr, 2ch, 1tr in next tr, 2ch, miss 1tr, 1tr in next tr, 1tr in each of next 2ch, 4ch); repeat to end, sl st into 3rd ch of 7, sl st across 2ch.

**Round 7**: 7ch, (1tr in each of next 2ch, 1tr in next tr, 2ch, miss 1tr, 1tr in next tr, * 2ch, 1tr in next tr; * repeat from * to * twice, 2ch, miss 1tr, 1tr in next tr, 1tr in 1ch, miss 1ch, 1tr in next tr, 2ch, miss 1tr,

1tr in next tr; repeat from * to * 3 times, 2ch, miss 1tr, 1tr in next tr, 1tr in each of next 2ch, 4ch); repeat to end, sl st into 3rd ch of 7, sl st across 2ch.

**Round 8**: 7ch, (1tr in each of next 2ch, 1tr in next tr, * 2ch, miss 1tr, 1tr in next tr, 1tr in 1ch, miss 1ch, 1tr in next tr, 2ch, 1tr in next tr, 2ch, 1tr in next tr, 2ch, 1tr in next tr, 1tr in 1ch, miss 1ch, 1tr in next tr; * repeat from * to * once, 2ch, miss 1tr, 1tr in next tr, 1tr in each of next 2ch, 4ch); repeat to end, sl st into 3rd ch of 7, sl st across 2ch.

**Round 9**: 7ch, (1tr in each of next 2ch, 1tr in next tr, * 2ch, miss 1tr, 1tr in next tr, 2ch, 1tr in next tr, 2ch, miss 1tr, 1tr in next tr, 1tr in 1ch, miss 1ch, 1tr in next tr, 2ch, 1tr in next tr, 1tr in 1ch, miss 1ch, 1tr in next tr; * repeat from * to * once, 2ch, miss 1tr, 1tr in next tr, 2ch, 1tr in next tr, 2ch, miss 1tr, 1tr in next tr, 1tr in each of next 2ch, 4ch); repeat to end, sl st into 3rd ch of 7, sl st across 2ch.

**Round 10**: 7ch, (1tr in each of next 2ch, 1tr in next tr, * 2ch, miss 1tr, 1tr in next tr, 2ch, 1tr in next tr, 2ch, 1tr in next tr, 2ch, 1tr in next tr, 2ch, miss 1tr, 1tr in next tr, 1tr in 1ch, miss 1ch, 1tr in next tr; * repeat from * to * once, 2ch, miss 1tr, 1tr in next tr, 2ch, 1tr in next tr, 2ch, 1tr in next tr, 2ch, 1tr in next tr, 2ch, miss 1tr, 1tr in next tr, 1tr in each of next 2ch, 4ch); repeat to end, sl st across 2ch. Continue to work blocks like this in all rounds. Refer to graph.

**Round 11**: 7ch, (1 block, 2ch, * 1 block, 2ch, 1tr in next tr, 2ch, 1tr in next tr, 2ch, 1 block, 2ch; * repeat from * to * twice, 1 block, 4ch); repeat to end, sl st into 3rd ch of 7, sl st across 2ch.

**Round 12**: 7ch, (1 block, * 2ch, 1tr in next tr, 2ch, 1tr in next tr, 2ch, 1 block, 2ch, 1 block; * repeat from * to * twice, 2ch, 1tr in next tr, 2ch, 1tr in next tr, 2ch, 1 block, 4ch); repeat to end, sl st into 3rd ch of 7, sl st across 2ch.

**Round 13**: 7ch, (1 block, * 2ch, 1tr in next tr; * repeat from * to * 3 times, 2ch, 1 block; repeat from * to * 4 times, 2ch, 1 block; repeat from * to * 4 times, 2ch, 1 block; repeat from * to * 4 times, 2ch, 1 block, 4ch); repeat to end, sl st into 3rd ch of 7, sl st across 2ch.

**Round 14**: 7ch, (1 block, * 2ch, 1 block, 2ch, 1tr in next tr, 2ch, 1tr in next tr, 2ch, 1 block; * repeat from * to * 3 times, 2ch, 1 block, 4ch); repeat to end, sl st into 3rd ch of 7, sl st across 2ch.

**Round 15**: 7ch, (1 block, * 2ch, 1tr in next tr, 2ch, 1tr in next tr, 2ch, 1 block, 2ch, 1 block; * repeat from * to * 3 times, 2ch, 1tr in next tr, 2ch, 1tr in next tr, 2ch, 1 block, 4ch); repeat to end, sl st into 3rd ch of 7, sl st across 2ch.

**Round 16**: 7ch, (1 block, * 2ch, 1tr in next tr; * repeat from * to * 3 times, ** 2ch, 1 block; repeat from * to * 4 times; ** repeat from ** to ** 3 times, 4ch); repeat to end, sl st into 3rd ch of 7, sl st across 2ch.

**Round 17**: 7ch, (1 block, * 2ch, 1 block, 2ch, 1tr in next tr, 2ch, 1tr in next tr, 2ch, 1 block; * repeat from * to * 4 times, 2ch, 1 block, 4ch); repeat to end, sl st into 3rd ch of 7, sl st across 2ch.

**Round 18**: 7ch, (1 block, * 2ch, 1tr in next tr, 2ch, 1tr in next tr, 2ch, 1 block, 2ch, 1 block; * repeat from * to * 4 times, 2ch, 1tr in next tr, 2ch, 1tr in next tr, 2ch, 1 block, 4ch); repeat to end, sl st into 3rd ch of 7, sl st across 2ch.

**Round 19**: 7ch, (1 block, * 2ch, 1tr in next tr; * repeat from * to * 3 times, ** 2ch, 1 block; repeat from * to * 4 times; ** repeat from ** to ** 4 times, 2ch, 1 block, 4ch); repeat to end, sl st into 3rd ch of 7, sl st across 2ch.

**Round 20**: 7ch, (1 block, * 2ch, 1 block, 2ch, 1tr in next tr, 2ch, 1tr in next tr, 2ch, 1 block; * repeat from * to * 5 times, 2ch, 1 block, 4ch); repeat to end, sl st into 3rd ch of 7, sl st across 2ch.

**Round 21**: 7ch, (1 block, * 2ch, 1tr in next tr, 2ch, 1tr in next tr, 2ch, 1 block, 2ch, 1 block; * repeat from * to * 5 times, 2ch, 1tr in next tr, 2ch, 1tr in next tr, 2ch, 1 block, 4ch); repeat to end, sl st into 3rd ch of 7, sl st across 2ch.

**Round 22**: 7ch, (1 block, * 2ch, 1tr in next tr; * repeat from * to * 3 times, ** 2ch, 1 block; repeat from * to * 4 times; ** repeat from ** to ** 5 times, 2ch, 1 block, 4ch); repeat to end, sl st into 3rd ch of 7, sl st across 2ch.

**Round 23**: 7ch, (1 block, * 2ch, 1 block, 2ch, 1tr in next tr, 2ch, 1tr in next tr, 2ch, 1 block; * repeat from * to * 6 times, 2ch, 1 block, 4ch); repeat to end, sl st into 3rd ch of 7, sl st across 2ch.

**Round 24**: 7ch, (1 block, * 2ch, 1tr in next tr, 2ch, 1tr in next tr, 2ch, 1 block, 2ch, 1 block; * repeat from * to * 6 times, 2ch, 1tr in next tr, 2ch, 1tr in next tr, 2ch, 1 block, 4ch); repeat to end, sl st into 3rd ch of 7, sl st across 2ch.

**Round 25**: 7ch, (1 block, * 2ch, 1tr in next tr; * repeat from * to * 3 times, ** 2ch, 1 block; repeat from * to * 4 times; ** repeat from ** to ** 6 times, 2ch, 1 block, 4ch); repeat to end, sl st into 3rd ch of 7, sl st across 2ch.

**Round 26**: 7ch, (1 block, 2ch, 1 block, 2ch, 1tr in next tr, 2ch, 1tr in next tr, 2ch, 1 block, * 2ch, 1tr in next tr; * repeat from * to * 35 times, 2ch, 1 block, 2ch, 1tr in next tr, 2ch, 1tr in next tr, 2ch, 1 block, 2ch, 1 block, 4ch); repeat to end, sl st into 3rd ch of 7, sl st across 2ch.

**Round 27**: 7ch, (1 block, 2ch, 1tr in next tr, 2ch, 1tr in next tr, 2ch, 1 block, 2ch, 1 block, * 2ch, 1tr in next tr; * repeat from * to * 37 times, 2ch, 1 block, 2ch, 1 block; repeat from * to * twice, 2ch,

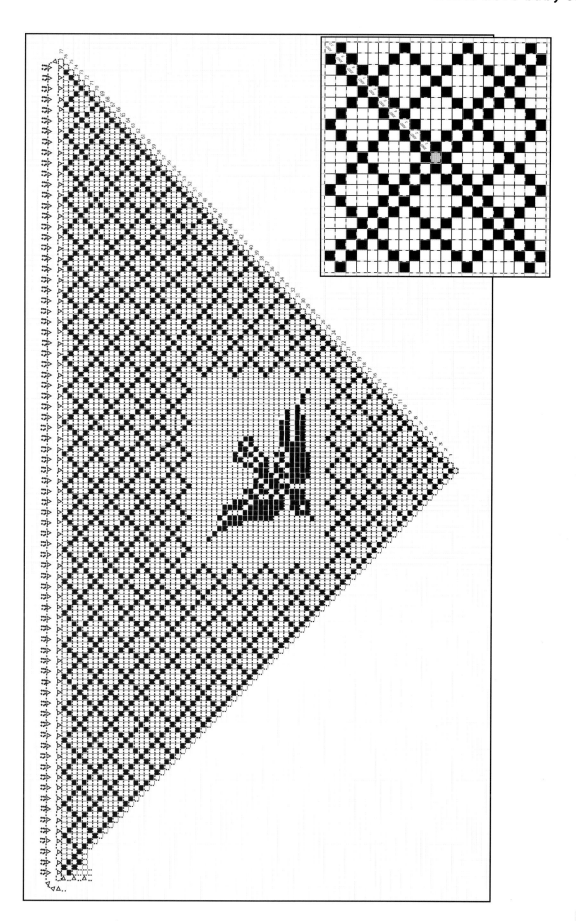

1 block, 4ch); repeat to end omitting last tr, sl st into 3rd ch of 7, sl st across 2ch.

**Round 28**: 7ch, ( 1 block, * 2ch, 1tr in next tr; * repeat from * to * 3 times, 2ch, 1 block; repeat from * to * 28 times, 2ch, 1 block; repeat from * to * 10 times, 2ch, 1 block; repeat from * to * 4 times, 2ch, 1 block, 4ch); repeat to end, omitting last tr, sl st into 3rd ch of 7, sl st across 2ch.

**Round 29**: 7ch, (1 block, 2ch, 1 block, 2ch, 1tr in next tr, 2ch, 1tr in next tr, 2ch, 1 block, 2ch, 1 block, * 2ch, 1tr in next tr; * repeat from * to * twice, 2ch, 1 block; repeat from * to * 10 times, 2ch, 1 block in each of next 5 spaces, [11 treble worked]; repeat from * to * 3 times, 2ch, work 1 block in each of next 3 spaces, [7 treble worked]; repeat from * to * 10 times, 2ch, 1 block, 2ch, 1 block; repeat from * to * twice, 2ch, 1 block, 2ch, 1 block, 4ch); repeat to end, omitting last tr, sl st into 3rd ch of 7, sl st across 2ch.

**Round 30**: 7ch, (1 block, * 2ch, 1tr in next tr; * repeat from * to * once, 2ch, 1 block, 2ch, 1 block; repeat from * to * twice, 2ch, 1 block; repeat from * to * 3 times, 2ch, 1 block in each of next 2 spaces [5 treble], 2ch, 1tr in next tr, 2ch, 1 block in each of next 7 spaces, 1tr in each of next 11 treble, 1 block [27 treble worked], 2ch, work 3 blocks [7 treble], miss 1tr, 2ch, 1 block; repeat from * to * 9 times, 2ch, 1 block; repeat from * to * twice, 2ch, 1 block, 2ch, 1 block; repeat from * to * twice, 2ch, 1 block, 4ch); repeat to end, omitting last tr, sl st into 3rd ch of 7, sl st across 2ch.

**Round 31**: 7ch, (1 block, * 2ch, 1tr in next tr; * repeat from * to * 3 times, 2ch, 1 block; repeat from * to * 4 times, 2ch, 1 block; repeat from * to * 4 times, 2ch, 1 block in each of next 2 spaces, 1tr in each tr of previous blocks, 2ch, work 5 blocks [11 treble]; repeat from * to * 8 times, 2ch, 1 block; repeat from * to * 4 times, 2ch, 1 block; repeat from * to * 4 times, 2ch, 1

block, 4ch); repeat to end sl st into 3rd ch of 7, sl st across 2ch.

**Round 32**: 7ch, (1 block, 2ch, 1 block, 2ch, 1tr in next tr, 2ch, 1tr in next tr, 2ch, 1 block, 2ch, 1 block, 2ch, 1tr in next tr, 2ch, 1tr in next tr, 2ch, 1 block, * 2ch, 1tr in next tr; * repeat from * to * 5 times, ** 2ch, miss 1tr, 1tr in next tr; ** repeat from ** to ** 5 times, 2ch, miss 1tr, work 8 blocks [17 treble], 2ch, work 4 blocks [9 treble]; repeat from * to * 10 times, 2ch, 1 block; repeat from * to * twice, 2ch, 1 block, 2ch, 1 block; repeat from * to * twice, 2ch, 1 block, 2ch, 1 block, 4ch); repeat to end, sl st into 3rd ch of 7, sl st across 2ch.

**Round 33**: 7ch, (1 block, * 2ch, 1tr in next tr; * repeat from * to * once, 2ch, 1 block, 2ch, 1 block; repeat from * to * twice, 2ch, 1 block, 2ch, 1 block; repeat from * to * 7 times, 2ch, work 8 blocks, 2ch, miss 1tr, 1tr in next tr, 2ch, miss 1tr, 1 block, 2ch, miss 1 tr, 1 block, 2ch, miss 1tr, 2 blocks, 2ch, miss 1tr, 1tr in next tr, 2ch, miss 1tr, 1tr in next tr, 2ch, miss 1tr, 1tr in next tr; repeat from * to * 11 times, 2ch, 1 block, 2ch, 1 block; repeat from * to * twice, 2ch, 1 block, 2ch, 1 block; repeat from * to * twice, 2ch, 1 block, 4ch); repeat to end, sl st into 3rd ch of 7, sl st across 2ch.

**Round 34**: 7ch, (1 block, * 2ch, 1tr in next tr; * repeat from * to * 3 times, 2ch, 1 block; repeat from * to * 4 times, 2ch, 1 block; repeat from * to * 9 times, 2ch, miss 1tr, 1tr in next tr, 2ch, miss 1tr, work 5 blocks [11 treble], 2ch, miss 1tr, work 2 blocks [5 treble], 2ch, miss 1tr, work 2 blocks [5 treble], 2ch, miss 2ch sp, 1 block, 2ch, miss 1tr, work 3 blocks [7 treble]; repeat from * to * 12 times, 2ch, 1 block; repeat from * to * 4 times, 2ch, 1 block; repeat from * to * 4 times, 2ch, 1 block, 4ch); repeat to end, sl st into 3rd ch of 7, sl st across 2ch.

**Round 35**: 7ch, (1 block, 2ch, 1 block, * 2ch, 1tr in next tr; * repeat from * to * once, 2ch, 1 block, 2ch,

1 block; repeat from * to * twice, 2ch, 1 block, 2ch, 1 block; repeat from * to * 10 times, * 2ch, miss 1tr, 1tr in next tr; * repeat from * to * 4 times, 2ch, miss 2ch sp, 1 block, 2ch, miss 1tr, work 2 blocks [5 treble], 2ch, miss 1tr, work 3 blocks [7 treble], 2ch, miss 1tr, work 3 blocks [7 treble]; repeat from * to * 10 times, 2ch, 1 block, 2ch, 1 block; repeat from * to * twice, 2ch, 1 block, 2ch, 1 block; repeat from * to * twice, 2ch, 1 block, 2ch, 1 block, 4ch); repeat to end, sl st into 3rd ch of 7, sl st across 2ch.

**Round 36**: 7ch, (1 block, ** 2ch, 1tr in next tr, 2ch, 1tr in next tr, 2ch, 1 block, 2ch, 1 block; ** repeat from ** to ** once, 2ch, 1tr in next tr, 2ch, 1tr in next tr, 2ch, 1 block * 2ch, 1tr in next tr; * repeat from * to * 14 times, 2ch, miss 2ch sp, 1tr in next tr, 2ch, miss 1tr, 1tr in next tr, 2ch, miss 2ch sp, 1tr in next tr, 2ch, miss 1tr, 1tr in next tr, 2ch, miss 1tr, work 3 blocks [7 treble], 2ch, miss 1tr, work 5 blocks [11 treble]; repeat from * to * 8 times, 2ch, 1 block; repeat from ** to ** twice, 2ch, 1tr in next tr, 2ch, 1tr in next tr, 2ch, 1 block, 4ch); repeat to end, sl st into 3rd ch of 7, sl st across 2ch.

**Round 37**: 7ch, (1 block, * 2ch, 1tr in next tr; * repeat from * to * 3 times, ** 2ch, 1 block; repeat from * to * 4 times; ** repeat from ** to ** once, 2ch, 1 block; repeat from * to * 14 times, 2ch, work 5 blocks [11 treble], 2ch, miss 1tr, 1 block, 2ch, miss 1tr, work 4 blocks; repeat from * to * 7 times; repeat from ** to ** 3 times, 2ch, 1 block, 4ch); repeat to end, sl st into 3rd ch of 7, sl st across 2ch.

**Round 38**: 7ch, (1 block, 2ch, ** 1 block, 2ch, 1tr in next tr, 2ch, 1tr in next tr, 2ch, 1 block, 2ch; ** repeat from ** to ** twice, 1tr in next tr, * 2ch, 1tr in next tr; * repeat from * to * 13 times, 2ch, 1 block, 2ch, miss 1tr, work 3 blocks [7 treble], 2ch, miss 1tr, work 2 blocks [5 treble], 2ch, miss 2ch sp, work 4 blocks [9 treble]; repeat from * to * 8 times, 2ch; repeat from ** to ** 3 times, 1 block, 4ch); repeat to end, sl st into 3rd ch of 7, sl st across 2ch.

**Round 39**: 7ch, (1 block, ** 2ch, 1tr in next tr, 2ch, 1tr in next tr, 2ch, 1 block, 2ch, 1 block; ** repeat from ** to ** twice, * 2ch, 1tr in next tr; * repeat from * to * 13 times, 2ch, 1 block, 2ch, miss 1tr, 1 block, 2ch, miss 1tr, 1 block, 2ch, miss 1tr, work 2 blocks [5 treble], 2ch, miss 1tr, work 5 blocks [11 treble]; repeat from * to * 9 times, 2ch, 1 block, 2ch, 1 block; repeat from ** to ** twice, 2ch, 1tr in next tr, 2ch, 1tr in next tr, 2ch, 1 block, 4ch); repeat to end, sl st into 3rd ch of 7, sl st across 2ch.

**Round 40**: 7ch, (1 block, * 2ch, 1tr in next tr; * repeat 3 times, ** 2ch, 1 block; repeat from * to * 4 times; ** repeat from ** to ** once, 2ch, 1 block; repeat from * to * 13 times, 2ch, work 2 blocks, 2ch, miss 1tr, 1 block, 2ch, miss 1tr, 1 block; repeat from * to * 3 times, 2ch, work 2 blocks, 2ch, miss 1tr, work 3 blocks; repeat from * to * 10 times; repeat from ** to ** 3 times, 2ch, 1 block, 4ch); repeat to end, sl st into 3rd ch of 7, sl st across 2ch.

**Round 41**: 7ch, (1 block, 2ch, ** 1 block, 2ch, 1tr in next tr, 2ch, 1tr in next tr, 2ch, 1 block, 2ch; ** repeat from ** to ** twice, 1 block, * 2ch, 1tr in next tr; * repeat from * to * 11 times, 2ch, 1 block, 2ch, miss 1tr, work 2 blocks, 2ch, miss 2ch sp, 1 block; repeat from * to * 3 times, 2ch, 1 block, 2ch, miss 1tr, 1 block, 2ch, miss 1tr, 2 blocks; repeat from * to * 9 times, 2ch, 1 block, 2ch; repeat from ** to ** 3 times, 1 block, 4ch); repeat to end, sl st into 3rd ch of 7, sl st across 2ch.

**Round 42**: 7ch, (1 block, 2ch, 1tr in next tr, 2ch, 1tr in next tr, 2ch, ** 1 block, 2ch, 1 block, 2ch, 1tr in next tr, 2ch, 1tr in next tr, 2ch; ** repeat from ** to ** twice, 1 block, * 2ch, 1 tr in next tr; * repeat from * to * 10 times, 2ch, miss 1tr, 2 blocks, 2ch, miss 1tr, 1 block; repeat from * to * 5 times, 2ch, miss 1tr, 1tr in next tr, 2ch, miss 2ch sp, 2 blocks, 2ch, miss 1tr, 2 blocks; repeat from * to * 7 times, 2ch, 1 block,

2ch, 1tr in next tr, 2ch, 1tr in next tr, 2ch; repeat from ** to ** 3 times, 1 block, 4ch); repeat to end, sl st into 3rd ch of 7, sl st across 2ch.

**Round 43**: 7ch, (1 block, ** 2ch, 1tr in next tr, 2ch, 1tr in next tr, 2ch, 1tr in next tr, 2ch, 1 tr in next tr, 2ch, 1 block; ** repeat from ** to ** 3 times, * 2ch, 1tr in next tr; * repeat from * to * 11 times, 2ch, miss 1tr, 1tr in next tr, 2ch, miss 1tr, 2 blocks; repeat from * to * 6 times, 2ch, 2 blocks, 2ch, 2 blocks; repeat from * to * 6 times, 2ch, 1 block; repeat from ** to ** 4 times, 4ch); repeat to end, sl st into 3rd ch of 7, sl st across 2ch.

**Round 44**: 7ch, (1 block, ** 2ch, 1 block, 2ch, 1tr in next tr, 2ch, 1tr in next tr, 2ch, 1 block; ** repeat from ** to ** 3 times, * 2ch, 1tr in next tr; * repeat from * to * 14 times, 2ch, miss 1tr, 1tr in next tr, 2ch, miss 1tr, 1tr in next tr; repeat from * to * 7 times, 2ch, miss 1tr, 1 block, 2ch, miss 2ch sp, 2 blocks; repeat from * to * 7 times; repeat from ** to ** 4 times, 2ch, 1 block, 4ch); repeat to end, sl st into 3rd ch of 7, sl st across 2ch.

**Round 45**: 7ch, (1 block, ** 2ch, 1tr in next tr, 2ch, 1tr in next tr, 2ch, 1 block, 2ch, 1 block; ** repeat from ** to ** 3 times, * 2ch, 1tr in next tr; * repeat from * to * 24 times, 2ch, work 2 blocks, 2ch, work 2 blocks; repeat from * to * 7 times, 2ch, 1 block, 2ch, 1 block; repeat from ** to ** 3 times, 2ch, 1tr in next tr, 2ch, 1tr in next tr, 2ch, 1 block, 4ch); repeat to end, sl st into 3rd ch of 7, sl st across 2ch.

**Round 46**: 7ch, (1 block, ** 2ch, 1tr in next tr, 2ch, 1tr in next tr, 2ch, 1tr in next tr, 2ch, 1 block; ** repeat from ** to ** 3 times, * 2ch, 1tr in next tr; * repeat from * to * 27 times, 2ch, 1 block, 2ch, 1 block; repeat from * to * 8 times, 2ch, 1 block; repeat from ** to ** 4 times, 4ch); repeat to end, sl st into 3rd ch of 7, sl st across 2ch.

**Round 47**: 7ch, (1 block, 2ch, 1 block, ** 2ch, 1tr in next tr, 2ch, 1tr in next tr, 2ch, 1 block, 2ch, 1 block; ** repeat from ** to ** 3 times, * 2ch, 1tr in next tr; * repeat from * to * 29 times, 2ch, 1 block; repeat from * to * 6 times, 2ch, 1 block, 2ch, 1 block; repeat from ** to ** 4 times, 4ch); repeat to end, sl st into 3rd ch of 7, sl st across 2ch.

**Round 48**: 7ch, (1 block, ** 2ch, 1tr in next tr, 2ch, 1tr in next tr, 2ch, 1 block, 2ch, 1 block; ** repeat from ** to ** 3 times, 2ch, 1tr in next tr, 2ch, 1tr in next tr, 2ch, 1 block, * 2ch, 1tr in next tr; * repeat from * to * 29 times, 2ch, 1 block; repeat from * to * 4 times, 2ch, 1 block; repeat from ** to ** 4 times, 2ch, 1tr in next tr, 2ch, 1tr in next tr, 2ch, 1 block, 4ch); repeat to end, sl st into 3rd ch of 7, sl st across 2ch.

**Round 49**: 7ch, (1 block, ** 2ch, 1tr in next tr, 2ch, 1tr in next tr, 2ch, 1tr in next tr, 2ch, 1tr in next tr, 2ch, 1 block; ** repeat from ** to ** 4 times, * 2ch, 1tr in next tr; * repeat from * to * 33 times, 2ch, 1 block; repeat from ** to ** 5 times, 4ch); repeat to end, sl st into 3rd ch of 7, sl st across ch.

**Round 50**: 7ch, (1 block, ** 2ch, 1 block, 2ch, 1tr in next tr, 2ch, 1tr in next tr, 2ch, 1 block; ** repeat from ** to ** 4 times, * 2ch, 1tr in next tr; * repeat from * to * 35 times; repeat from ** to ** 5 times, 2ch, 1 block, 4ch); repeat to end, sl st into 3rd ch of 7, sl st across 2ch.

**Round 51**: 7ch, (1 block, ** 2ch, 1tr in next tr, 2ch, 1tr in next tr, 2ch, 1 block, 2ch, 1 block; ** repeat from ** to ** 4 times, * 2ch, 1tr in next tr; * repeat from * to * 37 times, 2ch, 1 block, 2ch, 1 block; repeat from ** to ** 4 times, 2ch, 1tr in next tr, 2ch, 1tr in next tr, 2ch, 1 block, 4ch); repeat to end, sl st into 3rd ch of 7, sl st across 2ch.

**Round 52**: 7ch, (1 block, * 2ch, 1tr in next tr, 2ch, 1tr in next tr, 2ch, 1tr in next tr, 2ch, 1tr in next tr,

2ch, 1 block; * repeat from * to * 16 times, 4ch); repeat to end, sl st into 3rd ch of 7, sl st across 2ch.

**Round 53**: 7ch, (1 block, 2ch, * 1 block, 2ch, 1tr in next tr, 2ch, 1tr in next tr, 2ch, 1 block, 2ch; * repeat from * to * 16 times, 1 block, 4ch); repeat to end, sl st into 3rd ch of 7, sl st across 2ch.

**Round 54**: 7ch, (1 block, * 2ch, 1tr in next tr, 2ch, 1tr in next tr, 2ch, 1 block, 2ch, 1 block; * repeat from * to * 16 times, 2ch, 1 tr in next tr, 2ch, 1tr in next tr, 2ch, 1 block, 4ch); repeat to end, sl st into 3rd ch of 7, sl st across 2ch.

**Round 55**: 7ch, (1 block, * 2ch, 1tr in next tr, 2ch, 1tr in next tr, 2ch, 1tr in next tr, 2ch, 1tr in next tr, 2ch, 1 block; * repeat from * to * 17 times, 4ch); repeat to end, sl st into 3rd ch of 7, sl st across 2ch.

**Round 56**: 7ch, (1 block, 2ch, * 1 block, 2ch, 1tr in next tr, 2ch, 1tr in next tr, 2ch, 1 block, 2ch; * repeat from * to * 17 times, 1 block, 4ch); repeat to end, sl st into 3rd ch of 7, sl st across 2ch.

**Round 57**: 7ch, (1 block, * 2ch, 1tr in next tr, 2ch, 1 tr in next tr, 2ch, 1 block, 2ch, 1 block; * repeat from * to * 17 times, 2ch, 1tr in next tr, 2ch, 1tr in next tr, 2ch, 1 block, 4ch); repeat to end, sl st into 3rd ch of 7, sl st across 2ch.

**Round 58**: 7ch, (1 block, * 2ch, 1tr in next tr, 2ch, 1tr in next tr, 2ch, 1tr in next tr, 2ch, 1tr in next tr, 2ch, 1 block; * repeat from * to * 18 times, 4ch); repeat to end, sl st into 3rd ch of 7, sl st across 2ch.

**Round 59**: 7ch, (1 block, 2ch, * 1 block, 2ch, 1tr in next tr, 2ch, 1tr in next tr, 2ch, 1 block, 2ch, 1 block; * repeat from * to * 18 times, 4ch); repeat to end, sl st into 3rd ch of 7, sl st across 2ch.

**Round 60**: 7ch, (1 block, * 2ch, 1tr in next tr, 2ch, 1tr in next tr, 2ch, 1 block, 2ch, 1 block; * repeat from * to * 18 times, 2ch, 1tr in next tr, 2ch, 1tr in

next tr, 2ch, 1 block, 4ch); repeat to end, sl st into 3rd ch of 7, sl st across 2ch.

**Round 61**: 7ch, (1 block, * 2ch, 1tr in next tr, 2ch, 1tr in next tr, 2ch, 1tr in next tr, 2ch, 1tr in next tr, 2ch, 1 block; * repeat from * to * 19 times, 4ch); repeat to end, sl st into 3rd ch of 7, sl st across 2ch.

**Round 62**: 7ch, (1 block, 2ch, * 1 block, 2ch, 1tr in next tr, 2ch, 1tr in next tr, 2ch, 1 block, 2ch; * repeat from * to * 19 times, 1 block, 4ch); repeat to end, sl st into 3rd ch of 7, sl st across 2ch.

**Round 63**: 7ch, (1 block, * 2ch, 1tr in next tr, 2ch, 1tr in next tr, 2ch, 1 block, 2ch, 1 block; * repeat from * to * 19 times, 2ch, 1tr in next tr, 2ch, 1tr in next tr, 2ch, 1 block, 4ch); repeat to end, sl st into 3rd ch of 7, sl st across 2ch.

**Round 64**: 7ch, (1 block, * 2ch, 1tr in next tr, 2ch, 1tr in next tr, 2ch, 1tr in next tr, 2ch, 1 block; * repeat from * to * 20 times, 4ch); repeat to end, sl st into 3rd ch of 7, sl st across 2ch.

**Round 65**: 7ch, (1 block, 2ch, * 1 block, 2ch, 1tr in next tr, 2ch, 1tr in next tr, 2ch, 1 block, 2ch; * repeat from * to * 20 times, 1 block, 4ch); repeat to end, sl st into 3rd ch of 7, sl st across 2ch.

**Round 66**: 7ch, (1 block, * 2ch, 1tr in next tr, 2ch, 1tr in next tr, 2ch, 1 block, 2ch, 1 block; * repeat from * to * 20 times, 2ch, 1tr in next tr, 2ch, 1tr in next tr, 2ch, 1 block, 4ch); repeat to end, sl st into 3rd ch of 7, sl st across 2ch.

**Round 67**: 7ch, (1 block, * 2ch, 1tr in next tr, 2ch, 1tr in next tr, 2ch, 1tr in next tr, 2ch, 1tr in next tr, 2ch, 1 block; * repeat from * to * 21 times, 4ch); repeat to end, sl st into 3rd ch of 7, sl st across 2ch.

**Round 68**: 7ch, (1 block, 2ch, * 1 block, 2ch, 1tr in next tr, 2ch, 1tr in next tr, 2ch, 1 block, 2ch; *

repeat from * to * 21 times, 1 block, 4ch); repeat to end, sl st into 3rd ch of 7, sl st across 2ch.

**Round 69**: 7ch, (1 block, * 2ch, 1tr in next tr, 2ch, 1tr in next tr, 2ch, 1 block, 2ch, 1 block; * repeat from * to * 21 times, 2ch, 1tr in next tr, 2ch, 1tr in next tr, 2ch, 1 block, 4ch); repeat to end, sl st into 3rd ch of 7, sl st across 2ch.

**Round 70**: 7ch, (1 block, * 2ch, 1tr in next tr, 2ch, 1tr in next tr, 2ch, 1tr in next tr, 2ch, 1tr in next tr, 2ch, 1 block; * repeat from * to * 22 times, 4ch); repeat to end, sl st into 3rd ch of 7, sl st across 2ch.

**Round 71**: 7ch, (1 block, 2ch, * 1 block, 2ch, 1tr in next tr, 2ch, 1tr in next tr, 2ch, 1 block, 2ch; * repeat from * to * 22 times, 1 block, 4ch); repeat to end, sl st into 3rd ch of 7, sl st across 2ch.

**Round 72**: 7ch, (1 block, * 2ch, 1tr in next tr, 2ch, 1tr in next tr, 2ch, 1 block, 2ch, 1 block; * repeat from * to * 22 times, 2ch, 1tr in next tr, 2ch, 1tr in next tr, 2ch, 1 block, 4ch); repeat to end, sl st into 3rd ch of 7, sl st across 2ch.

**Round 73**: 7ch, (1 block, * 2ch, 1tr in next tr, 2ch, 1tr in next tr, 2ch, 1tr in next tr, 2ch, 1 block; * repeat from * to * 23 times, 4ch); repeat to end, sl st into 3rd ch of 7, sl st across 2ch.

**Round 74**: 7ch, (1 block, 2ch, * 1 block, 2ch, 1tr in next tr, 2ch, 1tr in next tr, 2ch, 1 block, 2ch; * repeat from * to * 23 times, 1 block, 4ch); repeat to end, sl st into 3rd ch of 7, sl st across 2ch.

**Round 75**: 7ch, (1 block, * 2ch, 1tr in next tr, 2ch, 1tr in next tr, 2ch, 1 block, 2ch, 1 block; * repeat from * to * 23 times, 2ch, 1tr in next tr, 2ch, 1tr in next tr, 2ch, 1 block, 4ch); repeat to end, sl st into 3rd ch of 7, sl st across 2ch.

**Round 76**: 7ch, (1 block, * 2ch, 1tr in next tr, 2ch, 1tr in next tr, 2ch, 1tr in next tr, 2ch, 1 block; * repeat from * to * 24 times, 4ch); repeat to end, sl st into 3rd ch of 7, sl st across 2ch.

**Round 77**: 7ch, 1 shell in corner sp, 2ch (1 shell in next sp, 2ch, miss 1sp); repeat to corner sp, 1 shell, 4ch, 1 shell into corner sp; repeat to end, sl st into 3rd ch of 7.

**Round 78**: edging shells are worked like this (3tr, 5ch, sl st into 3rd ch of 5 [a picot worked] 3tr into 2ch sp of next shell), work a shell into every 2ch space of previous shells to end. Fasten off.

# A winter throw

*This beautiful throw is simple to make. It is made from 100 per cent pure wool, so it is warm and snug, and will keep even the coldest person warm on chilly winter nights. This throw doubles as a bedspread — it easily fits a queen-sized bed.*

## Materials

Pure wool 8 ply
Maroon 45 × 50g balls
White 34 × 50g balls
Gold 80 × 50g balls

*Hook size*: 3.00 mm
*Tension*: 23 trebles to 10 cm (4 in) over flat work.

*Note*: For the bobble, work 5tr into next st, remove hook from loop, insert hook in first tr of 5tr group then back into loop and draw the loop through the tr, 1ch to fasten off.

Difficulty: *easy*

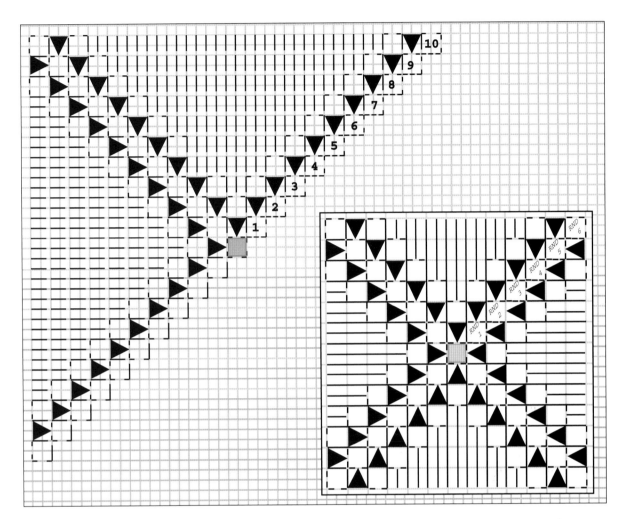

Ch8, sl st into first ch to form ring.

**Round 1**: 7ch, (1tr 1 bobble 1tr into ring, 4ch); repeat twice, 1tr 1 bobble into ring, omitting last tr, sl into 3rd ch of 7, sl st across 2ch.

**Round 2**: 7ch, (1tr 1 bobble into corner sp, 1tr in next tr, 2ch, 1tr in next tr, 1 bobble 1tr in corner sp, 4ch); repeat twice, 1tr 1 bobble in corner sp, 1tr in next tr, 2ch, 1tr in next tr 1 bobble in corner sp, omitting last tr, sl st into 3rd ch of 7, sl st across 2ch.

**Round 3**: 7ch, (1tr 1 bobble in corner sp, 1tr in next tr, 2ch, 1tr in next tr, 1tr in ch, miss 1ch, 1tr in next tr, 2ch, 1tr in next tr, 1 bobble 1tr in corner sp, 4ch); repeat to end, omitting last tr, sl st into 3rd ch of 7, sl st across 2ch.

**Round 4**: 7ch, (1tr 1 bobble in corner sp, 1tr in next tr, 2ch, 1tr in next tr, 1tr in ch, miss 1ch, 1tr in each of next 3tr, 1tr in ch miss 1ch, 1tr in next tr, 2ch, 1tr in next tr, 1 bobble 1tr in corner sp, 4ch); repeat to end, omitting last tr, sl st into 3rd ch of 7, sl st across 2ch.

**Round 5**: 7ch, (1tr 1 bobble into corner sp, 1tr in next tr, 2ch, 1tr in next tr, 1tr in ch, miss 1ch, 1tr in each of next 7tr, miss 1ch, 1tr in next ch, 1tr in next tr, 2ch, 1tr in next tr, 1 bobble 1tr in corner sp, 4ch); repeat to end, omitting last tr, sl st into 3rd ch of 7, sl st across 2ch.

**Round 6**: 7ch, (1tr 1 bobble into corner sp, 1tr in next tr, 2ch, 1tr in next tr, 1tr in ch, miss 1ch, 1tr in each of next 11tr, miss 1ch, 1tr in next ch, 1tr in next tr, 2ch, 1tr in next tr, 1 bobble 1tr in corner sp, 4ch);

repeat to end, omitting last tr, sl st into 3rd ch of 7, sl st across 2ch.

**Round 7**: 7ch, (1tr 1 bobble into corner sp, 1tr in next tr, 2ch, 1tr in next tr, 1tr in 1ch, miss 1ch, 1tr in each of next 15tr, miss 1ch, 1tr in next ch, 1tr in next tr, 2ch, 1tr in next tr, 1 bobble 1tr into corner sp, 4ch); repeat to end, omitting last tr, sl st into 3rd ch of 7, sl st across 2ch.

**Round 8**: 7ch, (1tr 1 bobble into corner sp, 1tr in next tr, 2ch, 1tr in next tr, 1tr in 1ch, miss 1ch, 1tr in each of next 19tr, miss 1ch, 1tr in next in ch, 1tr in next tr, 2ch, 1tr in next tr, 1 bobble 1tr into corner sp, 4ch); repeat to end, omitting last tr, sl st into 3rd ch of 7. Fasten off.

**Round 9**: 7ch, (1tr 1 bobble into corner sp, 1tr in next tr, 2ch, 1tr in next tr, 1tr in 1ch, miss 1ch, 1tr in each of next 23tr, 1tr in 1ch, miss 1ch, 1tr in next tr, 2ch, 1tr in next tr, 1 bobble 1tr into corner sp, 4ch); repeat to end, omitting last tr, sl st into 3rd ch of 7, sl st across 2ch.

**Round 10**: 7ch, (1tr 1 bobble into corner sp, 1tr in next tr, 2ch, 1tr in next tr, 1tr in 1ch, miss 1ch, 1tr in each of next 27tr, 1tr in 1ch, miss 1ch, 1tr in

next tr, 2ch, 1tr in next tr, 1 bobble 1tr into corner sp, 4ch); repeat to end, omitting last tr, sl st into 3rd ch of 7. Fasten off.

For the centre piece you will need to make 36 squares. For the round around the centre piece you will need to make 28 squares, and 4 squares of the same colour to go on the corners of the next round. For round 2, using a different colour, you will need to make 32 squares. For the last or outer round you will need to make 45 squares in the same colour as for round 2.

Join them by sewing the right sides together.

Work the edging in the same colour as the centre; join wool into a corner — work 1ch then 1dc in same sp, 4ch, work a bobble into the dc, (work 1dc into the 3rd tr from hook, 4ch, work a bobble into the dc); repeat to end.

Work around the edges of the throw, working 2 bobbles in corner spaces to end, work 1 bobble into the corner you started from and sl st into ch at start of round. Fasten off.

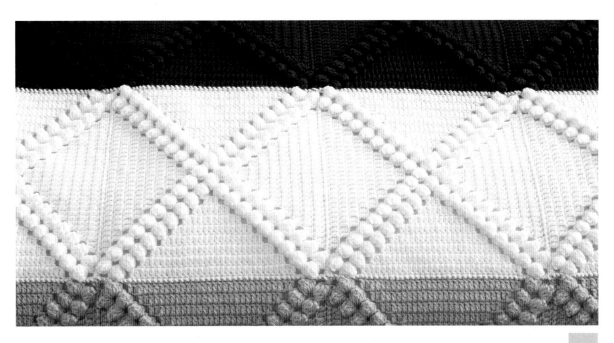

# Broncos
## baby blanket

*This blanket, which can also be used as a cot cover, is named after my favourite football team — their colours are maroon, white and gold. Of course, you can use different colour combinations, perhaps even matching that of your own favourite sporting team.*

## Materials

Pure wool 8 ply
White 30 × 50g balls
Gold 6 × 50g balls
Maroon 6 × 50g balls

*Hook size*: 3.00 mm
*Tension*: 17 trebles to 7.5 cm (3 in) over the last round of trebles on flat work.

*Note*: You will need to make 16 gold and white squares, 24 maroon and white squares and 74 plain white squares — 114 squares in total.

Difficulty: *medium*

To make gold and white squares start with gold wool and, 8ch, sl st into first ch to form ring.

**Round 1**: 7ch, (work 3tr into ring, 4ch) 3 times; and work 2tr into ring, sl st into 3rd ch of 7, this counts as a tr, sl st across 2ch.

**Round 2**: 7ch, (work 3tr into corner sp, 1tr in each of next 3tr, 3tr into corner sp [9 treble in all] 4ch); repeat to end, omitting last tr in corner sp, sl st into 3rd ch of 7.

**Round 3**: (work 1dc 6tr and 1dc into corner sp, miss 4tr, into the front loop of the 5th tr work 1dc, 6tr and 1dc, miss the next 4tr); repeat to end, sl st into dc of the first shell in corner sp. Fasten off.

Join white wool into the back loop of the 9th tr of round 2, this should be directly behind where you fastened off in round 3.

**Round 4**: 7ch, (work 1tr into the back loop of each next 9tr of round 2, 4ch); repeat to end, omitting 4ch, sl st into 3rd ch of 7, sl st across 2ch.

**Round 5**: 7ch, (work 1tr into each of next 2ch, 1tr into each of next 9tr and 1tr into each of next 2ch [13 treble worked in all], 4ch); repeat to end, omitting 4ch, sl st into 3rd ch of 7, sl st across 2ch.

**Round 6**: 7ch, (1tr into each of next 2ch, 1tr into each of next 13tr and 1tr into each of next 2ch [17 treble in all], 4ch); repeat to end, omitting 4ch, sl st into the 3rd ch of 7, sl st across 2ch.

**Round 7** is worked in gold. Ch6 (work 1dc into each of the next 2ch, 1dc into each of next 17tr and 1dc into each of next 2ch [21dc worked in all], 4ch); repeat to end, sl st into the first ch of 6. Fasten off.

Sew gold squares together with gold wool and maroon squares together with maroon wool.

Maroon and white squares are worked the same as gold and white squares, white squares are worked with 7 rounds worked in just white. Refer to photograph on page 54 for placement of squares.

Edging is worked in 1 round of gold and 1 round of maroon, join wool in corner sp.

Ch3, 1dc into each of next 2ch, 1dc into each dc and ch to corner, 2ch, 1dc into each dc along side of blanket working 2ch in the corners of the squares that protrude. Work in this manner all the way around, sl st into first ch of 3.

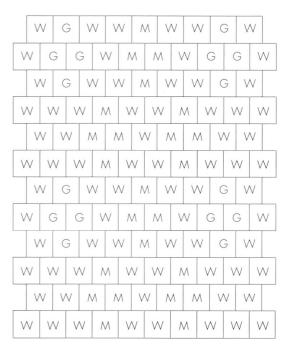

W = white
G = gold
M = maroon